TEAMBUILDING:

The ASTD Trainer's Sourcebook

Books in The ASTD Trainer's Sourcebook Series

TEAMBUILDING:

The ASTD Trainer's Sourcebook

**Cresencio Torres &
Deborah M. Fairbanks**

McGraw-Hill

New York   San Francisco   Washington D.C.   Auckland   Bogotá
Caracas   Lisbon   London   Madrid   Mexico City   Milan
Montreal   New Delhi   San Juan   Singapore
Sydney   Tokyo   Toronto

Library of Congress Catalog Number: 95-76444

McGraw-Hill

A Division of The **McGraw·Hill** Companies

9 10 11 12 13 14   MAL/MAL 8 7 6 5 4

ISBN 0-07-053435-7

Sourcebook Team:

Co-Publishers:	Philip Ruppel, Training McGraw-Hill
	Nancy Olson, American Society for Training and Development
Acquisitions Editor:	Richard Narramore, Training McGraw-Hill
Editing Supervisor:	Paul R. Sobel, McGraw-Hill Professional Book Group
Production Supervisor:	Pamela A. Pelton, McGraw-Hill Professional Book Group
Series Advisor:	Richard L. Roe
Editing/Imagesetting:	Claire Condra Arias, Stacy Marquardt, Ellipsys International Publications, Inc.
	Kalista Johnston-Nash

Acknowledgments

A special thanks to Dick Roe for his perseverance, Jerry Spiegel, Ph.D. for assisting in designing the *Organizational Team Readiness Survey* (OTRS) and the *Team Style Survey* (TSS), and to Roger Conway for assisting in the eleventh hour.

A special thanks to J.G. Alaksa for his additions to the book based on his vast experience in teambuilding and "just-in-time" training.

Contents

Preface

I'd like to tell you how this series came about. As a long-time editor and resource person in the training and development field, I was frequently asked by trainers, facilitators, consultants, and instructors to provide them with training designs on a variety of topics. These customers wanted one-hour, half-day, and full-day programs on such topics as teambuilding, coaching, diversity, supervision, and sales. Along with the training designs, they required facilitator notes, participant handouts, flipchart ideas, games, activities, structured experiences, overhead transparencies, and instruments. But, that wasn't all. They wanted to be able to reproduce, customize, and adapt these materials to their particular needs—at no cost!

Later, as an independent editor, I shared these needs with Nancy Olson, the publisher at the American Society for Training and Development. Nancy mentioned that ASTD received many similar calls from facilitators who were looking for a basic library of reproducible training materials. Many of the classic training volumes, such as Newstrom and Scannell's *Games Trainers Play* provided a variety of useful activities. However, they lacked training designs, handouts, overheads, and instruments—and, most importantly, they tended to be organized by method rather than by topic. You can guess the rest of the story: Welcome to *The ASTD Trainer's Sourcebook.*

This sourcebook is part of an open-ended series that covers the training topics most often found in many organizations. Instead of locking you into a prescribed "workbook mentality," this sourcebook will free you from having to buy more workbooks each time you present training. This volume contains everything you need—background information on the topic, facilitator notes, training designs, participant handouts, activities, instruments, flipcharts, overheads, and resources—and it's all reproducible! We welcome you to adapt it to your particular needs. Please read the copyright limitations on page iv, then photocopy . . . edit . . . add your name . . . add your client's name. Please don't tell us . . . it isn't necessary! Enjoy.

Richard L. Roe
ASTD Sourcebook Series Advisor

Chapter One:

Introduction

Welcome to *TEAMBUILDING: The ASTD Trainer's Sourcebook*—your one stop reference for teambuilding training materials. You can use these materials "as is" or customize them in anyway you wish to meet your specific needs.

> ### CHAPTER OVERVIEW
>
> This chapter serves three purposes:
>
> - First, it provides a rationale for teambuilding.
>
> - Second, it discusses the teambuilding process.
>
> - Third, it provides a description of the contents of the book and how the various parts relate to one another.

So, let's get started!

Rationale for Teambuilding

In organizations throughout the world, smart business leaders are moving away from the traditional work structures that stifle creativity, innovation, and change. These leaders are redesigning work to include teams at all levels of their organizations. They are realizing that teams offer many advantages over the more traditional ways of organizing the workforce. In using teams, skills and tasks are widely distributed among all team members. Also, team members are held accountable for maintaining and improving the processes for which their team is responsible. Finally, team members share leadership and management responsibilities.

Although the concept of teambuilding has changed over the years, the need for a comprehensive method for ensuring effective team development has increased. The flat, lean, team-based structures of high-involvement workplaces are being developed with an urgency unmatched in recent history.

Teambuilding reflects the need to change the way we do business so that employees are more motivated to contribute to the business. In addition, the synergy that comes from putting individuals together to form teams to solve problems, make decisions, and initiate action is power that must be harnessed for continued organizational success. When the team is working in such a way, we clearly recognize that within any team, "the whole is greater than the sum of its parts."

Why is teambuilding so important? As managers will verify, teambuilding works. It's that simple. Teambuilding helps members build on their strengths and minimize their weaknesses. It encourages them to manage their differences together, and it promotes a better understanding between individuals—the most critical factor in the success of any organization.

In the final analysis, teambuilding is the single most important tool that can bring a team together in the pursuit of common goals.

Six Reasons for Teambuilding

The six reasons for teambuilding are as follows:

1. To establish team purpose.

2. To understand the stages of team development.

3. To analyze how the team works based on team member roles.

4. To develop effective team communication.

5. To examine team processes.

6. To understand team leadership.

Because most teambuilding efforts revolve around these six issues, they will be the focus of the teambuilding sourcebook.

Understanding the Teambuilding Process

The teambuilding process is both dynamic and interactive. It requires creativity and flexibility in order to be successful. It is a process in which team members develop and improve working relationships and team functions. Teambuilding efforts vary, but most involve custom design interventions that are specific to individual team needs.

The process of teambuilding involves constant change. Yet, successful interventions can often be replicated in their original design because of recognized team dynamics, tasks, member roles, leader issues, and goals. Starting with a good design is important but what is most important is the ability to change with the needs of the team during the teambuilding session.

Teambuilding is a process that allows team members to begin to understand the nature of group dynamics in regards to effective teamwork and allows individuals to develop ways to increase team efficiency.

Sourcebook Organization

This sourcebook is organized into four specific parts. The first part lays the foundation of your teambuilding training with an introduction to the material and background information. The second involves getting ready to train—preparing facilities, materials, supplies, etc. The third consists of the actual teambuilding sessions. The fourth contains the learning activities, assessments, handouts and overhead transparencies used in the sessions.

Laying the foundation

1. Introduction

This chapter provides a rationale for teambuilding, provides an overview of the contents of this sourcebook, and provides a strategy for using the material most effectively.

2. Background

Chapter 2 provides background information about eight topics that will be discussed in the actual teambuilding sessions.

- Team Purpose
- Stages of Team Development
- Team Member Roles
- Team Communication
- Decision Making
- Problem Solving
- Managing Team Conflicts
- Self-Authorized Team Leadership

Administration issues

3. Planning the Workshop

The next chapter focuses on two aspects of workshop preparation and organization:

- Workshop Preparation

  Tips for managing your training program successfully—from facilitator preparation to workshop follow-up.

- Administrative Materials

  This chapter includes masters checklists for materials, supplies, arrangement of facilities, class roster, name tents, and a workshop completion certificate.

Training plans

The next three chapters cover the actual training activities themselves—complete with facilitator notes for the three events.

These training plans are designed to work together to make up a comprehensive set of teambuilding workshops. However, each can stand alone as a workshop if you so choose.

4. One-Hour Teambuilding Workshop

A complete training design for a one-hour teambuilding exercise.

5. Half-Day Teambuilding Workshop

A complete training plan for a half-day workshop stressing four key team development areas.

6. One-Day Teambuilding Workshop

A complete training plan for a one-day workshop stressing six key team development areas.

Training resources and materials

Chapters 7, 8, 9, and 10 contain the resources and materials upon which the workshops are based.

7. Participant Handouts

A collection of content-focused handouts that provide information for the topics covered in the sessions.

8. Learning Activities

A collection of activities, including instructions and handouts, that provide a foundation for active participant involvement.

9. Tools and Assessments

A short collection of simple assessments. Applied and discussed properly, these assessments set the stage for continued learning.

10. Overhead Transparencies

A collection of transparency masters designed for use with each of the three sessions. You can enhance or change them to meet your particular training needs.

Getting the Most from This Material

In order to present these workshops, you will need to become familiar with the contents of this book. Here is a suggested approach:

- Review Chapter 7 "Participant Handouts" to familiarize yourself with the content of the workshop. This will give you a good sense for how to plan the workshop.

- Review Chapter 8 "Learning Activities" to see the range of activities that can be part of the sessions.

- Review Chapter 9 "Tools and Assessments" to get an idea of what is available.

- Review Chapter 10 "Overhead Transparencies" to see how you can organize your material.

Having accomplished the above, move to the front of the book and review the three training designs to see how they are structured and how they can work together to create a truly outstanding teambuilding training program

Workshop Building Blocks

In this sourcebook, you have all the building blocks needed to create your own teambuilding training programs. The following pages provide a *Subject/Reference Matrix* to help you select the building blocks that fit your objectives.

Directions

To use the *Subject/Reference Matrix* on pages 8 through 11, follow the steps below:

1. To locate sourcebook material on a specific topic, go to Column A (Topic) and find the row that lists the topic needed. For example, if you want material on "Team Purpose," go to Column A, Row 1(Cell A-1).

2. Refer to the cells in the selected row to find page references for information and materials on the topic. For example, to locate learning activities on "Team Member Roles," go across Row 3 to the cell where the topic intersects with the "Learning Activities" column (Cell F-3).

3. Review the materials listed in Cell F-3, and select those that are appropriate for your group and time block.

4. Also, refer to the Appendix, *Recommended Resources*, for titles of additional material that meets your requirements.

Subject/Reference Matrix

A. Topic	B. Background	C. Scripts	D. Handouts	E. Overheads	F. Learning Activities	G. Tools and Assessments
1. Team Purpose	Defining Your Team's Mission (p. 16) Mission Formulation (p. 17) Operating Principles (p. 19) Team Goals (p. 20-21)	Team Purpose (pp. 116-119)	Team Purpose (p. 146) Team Mission (p. 147) Writing a Mission Statement (pp. 148-150) Team Goals (p. 151)	Team Mission (p. 234) Eight Criteria for Effective Mission Statements (p. 235) Mission Formulation (p. 236) Team Goals (p. 237) Goal Characteristics (p. 238)	Team Purpose (pp. 190-191)	Team Building Instrument (TBI) (pp. 215-220)
2. Team Development	Stages of Team Development (pp. 22-27) Theories of Group Development (p. 28)	Stages of Team Development (Half-Day) (pp. 90-92) Stages of Team Development (One-Day) (pp. 120-122)	Reasons for Teambuilding (p. 144) Effective Team Characteristics (p. 145) Stages of Team Development (pp. 152-156) Theories of Group Development (p. 157)	Stages of Team Development (p. 239) Forming Stage (p. 240) Storming Stage (p. 241) Norming Stage (p. 242) Performing Stage (p. 243)	What Team Stage Are We Going Through? (pp. 192-194)	Organizational Team Readiness Survey (OTRS) (pp. 206-214) Team Building Instrument (TBI) (pp. 215-220) Team Style Survey (TSS) (pp. 221-227) Team Development Rating Form (pp. 230-231)

Subject/Reference Matrix

A. Topic	B. Background	C. Scripts	D. Handouts	E. Overheads	F. Learning Activities	G. Tools and Assessments
3. Team Member Roles	Team Member Roles (p. 29-32)	Team Member Roles (Half-Day) (pp. 93-96) Team Member Roles (One-Day) (pp. 123-125)	Team Member Roles (pp. 158-161)	Team Member Roles (p. 244) Task Roles (p. 245) Process Roles (p. 246)	Team Values (pp. 200-201)	Team Building Instrument (TBI) (pp. 215-220)
4. Team Communication	Team Communication (pp. 35-36) Task Communication (p. 37) Process Communication (p. 38) Effective Team Communication (pp. 39-41)	Team Communication (Half-Day) (pp. 97-100) Team Communication (One-Day) (pp. 126-129)	Team Communication (pp. 163-166)	Communication Process (p. 249) Task Communication (p. 251) Task Communication Is . . . (p. 251) Process Communication (p. 252) Process Communication Is . . . (p. 253) Communication Barriers (p. 254) Overcoming Communication Barriers (p. 255)	Team Interaction Activity (Sociogram) (pp. 195-197)	Team Building Instrument (TBI) (pp. 215-220)

Subject/Reference Matrix

A. Topic	B. Background	C. Scripts	D. Handouts	E. Overheads	F. Learning Activities	G. Tools and Assessments
5. Feedback	Giving and Receiving Feedback (p. 42-45)		Giving Feedback to Others (pp. 167-168) Receiving Feedback from Others (p. 169)	Benefits of Giving Feedback (p. 256) Giving Feedback to Others (p. 257) Receiving Feedback from Others (p. 258)	Feedback Activity (pp. 202-204)	
6. Decision Making	Making Decisions (pp. 46-49)	Decision Making/ Problem Solving (pp. 130-133)	Decision Making (pp. 170-172)	The Difference Between Decision Making and Problem Solving (p. 259) Types of Decisions (p. 260) A Decision Model (p. 261) Decision-Making Procedures (p. 262)		
7. Problem Solving	Solving Problems (pp. 50-51)	Decision Making/ Problem Solving (pp. 130-133)	Problem Solving (p. 173)	The Difference Between Decision Making and Problem Solving (p. 259) Problem-Solving Steps (p. 263)		

Subject/Reference Matrix

A. Topic	B. Background	C. Scripts	D. Handouts	E. Overheads	F. Learning Activities	G. Tools and Assessments
8. Managing Team Conflict	Managing Team Conflict (pp. 52-54) Dysfunctional Team Member Behaviors (pp. 33-34)	Managing Team Conflict (Half-Day) (pp.101-104) Managing Team Conflict (One-Day) (pp.134-137)	Dysfunctional Team Member Behaviors (p. 162) Managing Team Conflict (p. 174)	Dysfunctional Team Member Behaviors (p. 247) Responses to Dysfunctional Behavior (p. 248) Causes of Team Conflict (p. 264) Conflict Management Strategies (p. 265) Conflict Resolution Approaches (pp. 266-270) Steps to Managing Team Conflict (p. 271)		
9. Self-Authorized Leadership	Self-Authorized Team Leadership (p. 56) Behavioral Strategies (p. 57) Congitive Strategies (p. 58) Increasing Effectiveness (p. 59) The Seven Pillars of Leadership Character (p. 60)	Self-Authorized Team Leadership (pp. 138-141)	Self-Authorized Team Leadership (pp. 181-183) Increasing Effectiveness (pp. 184-186) Leadership Character (pp. 187-188)	Self-Authorized Team Leadership (p. 272) Behavioral Strategies (p. 273) Cognitive Strategies (p. 274) Increasing Leadership Effectiveness (p. 275) The Seven Pillars of Leadership Character (p. 276)	Team Leadership: Finish the Sentence (pp. 198-199)	Team Building Instrument (TBI) (pp. 215-220) Leadership Role Checklist (pp. 228-229)

Navigating the Training Plans

The training plan is the key to each of the workshop sessions. These plans are set out in detail on a module-by-module basis, with a purpose, objectives, and agenda for each module. We have attempted to make these training plans as easy to use as possible.

- Each section within a module has a heading that includes a statement of purpose for the section and suggested timing.

- Within each section, you will find one or more major activities.

- In addition, you will find a number of supporting activities where appropriate.

- Suggested actions are shown in conjunction with supporting activities—in italics with the appropriate action verb in bold.

- Suggested comments accompany many of the suggested actions. These comments are not designed to be used as a script but rather thoughts that you can translate into your own words.

- At appropriate points, you will find places to make notes and comments about the material and the group with which you are working.

Understanding the Icons

Major activities

The following icons mark major activities:

Activities that feature facilitator commentary. In these activities, you—as facilitator—present information that will be key to subsequent workshop activities.

Activities carried out in small groups. You assign participants to small groups to complete the activity at hand. This icon is also used as a signal to listen for specific comments.

Activities that revolve around total training group discussion. Such activities typically follow major exercises on which participants have worked individually or in groups.

Activities to be completed on an individual basis.

Supporting activities

The following icons mark supporting activities:

An overhead transparency is to be shown. The title of the overhead transparency is referenced in the text accompanying the icon.

A participant handout, part or all of a learning activity, or an assessment is to be handed out.

A question is to be asked. Wording for the question is provided, as are suggested answers when appropriate.

A flipchart is to be used. If the flipchart is one of the "prepared flipcharts" recommended for the workshop, its title will appear in the accompanying text.

Notes

The following icons mark notes to the facilitator:

Indicates a special note or suggested pre-work.

Indicates when to call time for timed exercises.

Marks the end of an exercise or section.

Sample Page

section heading

timing

icons

suggested comments

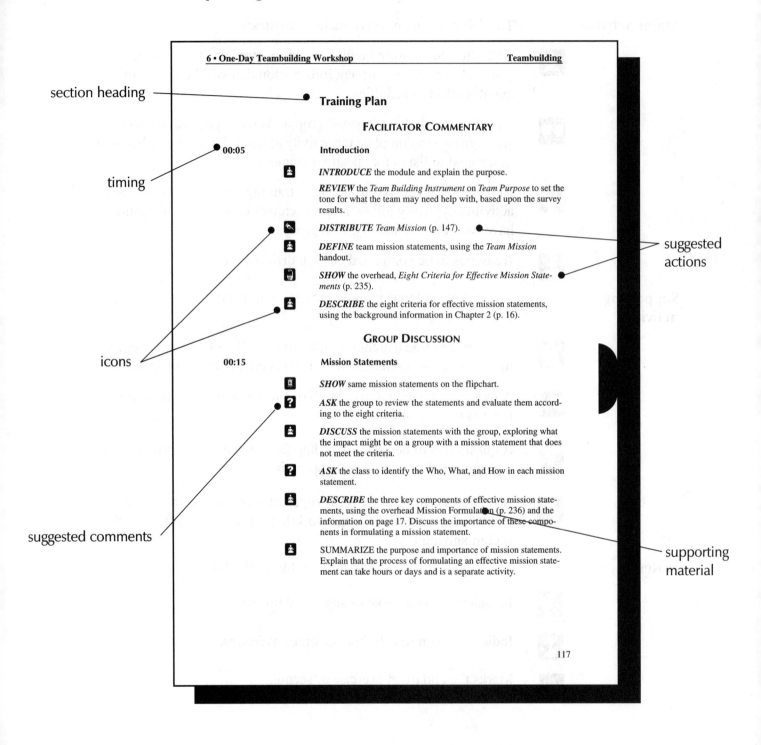

6 • One-Day Teambuilding Workshop   **Teambuilding**

Training Plan

FACILITATOR COMMENTARY

00:05   **Introduction**

INTRODUCE the module and explain the purpose.

REVIEW the *Team Building Instrument* on *Team Purpose* to set the tone for what the team may need help with, based upon the survey results.

DISTRIBUTE *Team Mission* (p. 147).

DEFINE team mission statements, using the *Team Mission* handout.

SHOW the overhead, *Eight Criteria for Effective Mission Statements* (p. 235).

DESCRIBE the eight criteria for effective mission statements, using the background information in Chapter 2 (p. 16).

GROUP DISCUSSION

00:15   **Mission Statements**

SHOW same mission statements on the flipchart.

ASK the group to review the statements and evaluate them according to the eight criteria.

DISCUSS the mission statements with the group, exploring what the impact might be on a group with a mission statement that does not meet the criteria.

ASK the class to identify the Who, What, and How in each mission statement.

DESCRIBE the three key components of effective mission statements, using the overhead Mission Formulation (p. 236) and the information on page 17. Discuss the importance of these components in formulating a mission statement.

SUMMARIZE the purpose and importance of mission statements. Explain that the process of formulating an effective mission statement can take hours or days and is a separate activity.

117

suggested actions

supporting material

Chapter Two:

Background

This chapter offers background information on the topics that are covered in the one-hour, half-day, and one-day workshops.

CHAPTER OVERVIEW

The more familiar you are with the material contained in this chapter, the easier it will be to conduct successful training. To get the most from this material:

- Read all the material before you begin any of the workshops.

- Define participant needs for teambuilding training.

- Adjust the material to fit participant needs.

- Prepare for the session.

Team Purpose and Mission

A team's purpose is defined by its mission. The team mission is something that the team intends to do. It is the object for which the team exists as determined by the team leader and team members. It is a clearly stated purpose that serves to direct and motivate the team in pursuit of its goals.

The team's mission is driven by the organization's vision. The organization's vision provides a "big picture" perspective that serves to align people, ideas, and attitudes. The organizational vision may be as vague as a dream or as clear as a specific outcome. It must, however, be communicated to team members in such a way that they are inspired to be part of it. To be successful, the team must align its purpose or mission to the organization's vision.

Defining Your Team's Mission

Effective teams are driven by an inspiring mission that must technically support the organization's vision of a desired future state. The mission, best expressed in writing, states the team's intended direction and acts as a guide to direct all of the team's efforts.

Eight criteria of effective mission statements

A clearly articulated mission provides the foundation for developing goals and action plans that will assist the team in reaching its desired outcome. In addition, it provides the team with the basis for determining what decisions must be made and the possible methods for finding workable solutions. Tom Peters describes eight criteria of effective mission statements. The mission statement must be:

1. **Inspirational.**

   It must provide an uplifting idea about what the team can ideally become.

2. **Clear and challenging.**

   It must describe a clear future state, not simply a description of the current situation.

3. **Differentiating.**

   It must describe the "uniqueness" of the team and how it can position itself as being distinctly different from the competition.

4. **Stable but constantly challenged.**

   It must provide direction and stability over time, adjusting as required to account for changes in the environment.

5. **Beacons and controls.**

   It must provide understanding of basic values and direction so that people can live it with unswerving consistency.

6. **Empowering.**

   It must help to draw forth the best from people.

7. **Future oriented.**

   It must assist in establishing commitment, confidence, and new direction.

8. **Lived in details, not broad strokes.**

   It must focus the day-to-day actions and set the current situation in motion toward a preferred future.

Mission Formulation

Mission formulation is a task that should involve all team members. When everyone on the team contributes to the process, there is a collective sense of accomplishment and a high level of commitment.

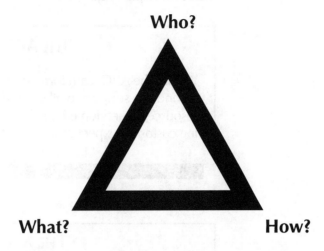

Elements of a mission statement

The mission statement must contain three key elements:

- What does the team do?
- For whom does the team perform its functions?
- How does the team go about doing its job?

What does the team do?

This element defines the purpose of the team. It specifies what the team does, the nature of the team's business, and why the team exists. It must be determined unanimously by all team members otherwise the team will unravel and eventually fall apart.

For whom does the team perform its functions?

This element defines who the primary customer is that the team serves. It identifies who will receive the benefits of the team's output. There should be interaction with the identified customer and discussion about how the team can meet the customer's needs.

How does the team go about doing its job?

Operating principles are the foundation of how team members get things done. They are based on stated values that guide the way team members work with each other. They are determined by examining individual values in relation to other team member values. This examination of values contributes to the establishment of a set of team-stated principles that will serve to guide how the team operates on a day-to-day basis.

Sample mission statements

The mission statement is a combination of specific facts that are integrated with parts of the organization's vision. It must be realistic and in line with the organization's resources and personnel. It must be compelling and attainable. An unrealistic mission statement that cannot be acted upon, only serves to undermine morale and team leadership.

THE ABC TEAM

We are the ABC team formed to provide quality information technology support to all customers, concentrating our resources on regional branches, and our efforts on exceeding customer expectations.

THE XYZ TEAM

We, the XYZ team, provide training and staff assistance in state-of-the-art management technologies to our internal clients, facilitating the successful transformation of organizational activities to a quality focused systems-oriented organization.

THE ALPHA TEAM

The mission of Alpha team is to provide responsive quality worldwide transportation and financial services in the most efficient and effective manner to satisfy customer requirements and expectations.

Operating Principles

In establishing operating principles, each team member is given the opportunity to share his or her personal values and beliefs about what is important to them as individual contributors. A composite of stated values becomes the shared values of the team if they are agreed upon. The operating principles become its valued working philosophy or something to live and work by.

OPERATING PRINCIPLES

We will:

• Work together to solve conflicts.

• Encourage dialogue with each other and listen to under-stand.

• Treat each other fairly and with respect.

• Maintain a safe and drug-free work environment.

The team's operating principles must be in alignment with organizational values that drive the way the business is accomplished.

Determining the team's operating principles is an important step in the teambuilding process. It requires an in-depth analysis of the most fundamental beliefs that underlie the way the team operates. But without clarifying individual values in relation to other team member values, misunderstandings will continually surface in team dynamics.

Once team members successfully clarify and discuss what is important to them, learn to appreciate their differences, and respect the others' belief systems, the team can move forward to accomplish its tasks with relative ease.

Team Goals

> ### EFFECTIVE GOALS ARE:
>
> - Specific.
> - Measurable.
> - Attainable.
> - Relevant.
> - Time bound.

A team goal is an end that the team strives to reach; it directly supports both the mission of the team and the organization's vision. Teams that agree on their agendas can direct their energies toward task accomplishment.

Effective team goals are determined by all team members. When everyone takes part in establishing the overall goals of the team, individuals on the team have a clear understanding of what is expected and can develop a commitment to working with one another in pursuit of team goals.

Common goals provide team members with:

- **Purpose**

  What needs to be done?

- **Clarity**

  What does the outcome look like?

- **Direction**

  What path must be followed?

Characteristics of Effective Goals

To be effective, goals must have certain characteristics. They must be specific, measurable, attainable, relevent, and time bound.

Specific

Goals must be easily understood. They must tell specifically what the team will accomplish.

Measurable

Goals must be measurable. They must be easily measured so that there is no question as to whether the team is successful or not in reaching the goals.

Attainable

Goals must be attainable. They must not be too difficult or too easy. If the goal is too challenging, the team may be frustrated if they cannot reach it. If the goal is not challenging enough, the team may not be motivated to accomplish it.

Relevant

Goals must be relevant. They must be congruent with the organization's stated desired future state and the team's mission.

Time Bound

Goals must be time bound. They must be guided by specific time parameters and deadlines for completion.

Goals provide focus and direction for good teamwork. They specify the direction needed for the effective utilization of team resources. Without common goals, the team will be unproductive and eventually flounder. Common agreed-upon goals serve to motivate team members to achieve success.

Stages of Team Development

When a group of people are first formed into a team, their roles and interactions are not established. Some individuals may merely act as observers while they try to determine what is expected from them while others may engage the process immediately. Gradually, the process of team development occurs, as team members understand their roles, find ways to work with one another, and learn about team issues.

There are many models that describe team developmental progression. They are all similar and suggest that the process occurs in four predictable stages. The four stages are:

- Forming

- Storming

- Norming

- Performing

Each stage is characteristically different and builds on the preceding one. The implication is that all teams must develop through this predetermined sequence if they are to be fully functioning teams. In addition, teams cycle through the stages over and over depending on the make-up of the team and the issues that they identify.

Forming

The forming stage of team development is an exploration period. Team members are often cautious and guarded in their interactions, not really knowing what to expect from other team members. They explore the boundaries of acceptable behavior and look for norms and roles that they are willing to support. Behaviors expressed in this early stage are generally polite and noncommittal.

While initial introductions are made, team members form opinions of others. There is a comparison of similarities and a close look at differences. First impressions often have a lasting effect on inter-personal relationships within the team but can change if team members show a willingness to engage in developing their relationships over the life span of the team.

Sometimes confusion and anxiety are experienced as individual differences surface within the team. When this occurs, team members attempt to establish safe patterns for interacting with each other.

Addressing the issue of inclusion

Each member is working on the issue of inclusion and making decisions as to whether they want to belong to the team or not. Some questions raised during this stage of development are:

* Do I want to be part of this team?

* Will I be accepted as a member?

* What price must I pay to belong to this team?

* Who is the leader?

* Is the leader competent?

There is a tendency during this stage for team members to rely heavily on the formal leadership of the group because of confusion and anxiety that individuals may experience.

In the forming stage, team productivity is low and relationships are guarded. Facilitators can guide the team through this stage by using the following guidelines:

* Share relevant information.

* Encourage open dialogue.

* Provide structure.

* Direct team issues.

* Develop a climate of trust and respect.

Storming

The storming stage of development is characterized by competition and strained relationships among team members. There are various degrees of conflict that teams experience but basically the storming stage deals with issues of power, leadership, and decision making. Conflict cannot be avoided during this phase. It is the most crucial stage that the team must work through.

In this stage, team members challenge differences in attempts to regain their individuality and influence. The discrepancy between what is expected of the team and what actually occurs in the process leads to frustration and anger. Some team members openly resist attempts to define team tasks or processes as they are presented. Sub-groups may form and polarize competing with other sub-groups for team influence.

The leadership issue is one of counter-dependence. Team members openly challenge the wisdom of the designated leadership and the leader's position. The leader is tested and challenged both overtly and covertly.

Because of the natural tendency to "circle the wagons" during times of conflict, team members may resort to non-supportive behaviors that they have relied upon in the past to manage conflict situations. They often fail to see the unique abilities and contributions made by other team members during this period.

The psychological notion of "fight" or "flight" manifests itself during this strained phase of team development. Team members either engage actively in the process or disengage due to the intensity of team member interactions. Working toward task accomplishment is paramount and relationship building sometimes takes a back seat to team collaboration.

Addressing the issue of control

Each member is addressing the issue of control and determining whether it is safe to be a member of the team. Some questions raised during this stage of development are:

- How will I seek my autonomy?

- How much control will I have over others?

- How much control will others try to have over me?

- Who do I support?

- Who supports me?

- How much influence do I have in this team?

The team must work through the conflict stage, or it will find itself unable to develop into a fully functional team. In addition, the team will continue to cycle back to the forming stage until team members resolve control issues experienced in the storming stage of development.

In the storming stage, team productivity still remains low but the energy of the team is high. Facilitators can guide the team through this stage by using the following guidelines:

- Engage team members in joint problem solving.

- Establish norms for looking at different view points.

- Discuss decision-making procedures.

- Encourage two-way communication.

- Support collaborative team efforts.

Norming

The norming stage of team development is characterized by cohesiveness among team members. After working through the storming stage, team members discover that they in fact do have common interests with each other. They learn to appreciate their differences, problem solve together, and feel more harmonious as a team.

At this time, the team starts to become a cohesive unit, and team members attempt to renegotiate their roles and the process for accomplishing the team's task.

Team members are now committed to working with other team members. Functional relationships have developed, and leadership issues are resolved through interdependent behavior. Trust, the most essential ingredient in team dynamics, begins to evolve.

Addressing the issue of solidarity

Each member is working on the issue of team solidarity. Some questions raised during this stage of development are:

- What kind of relationships can we develop?

- Will we be successful as a team?

- How do we measure up to other teams?

- What is my relationship to the team leader?

By the end of this stage, team members discover that they have more in common with one another. They learn to appreciate each other and have a heightened sense of belonging. The animosity toward the leader and other team members experienced in the storming stage decreases and normal, healthy, interpersonal relationships develop.

In this stage, team productivity increases and relationships based on trust develop. Facilitators can guide the team through this stage by using the following guidelines:

- Talk openly about issues and concerns.

- Encourage members to manage the team process.

- Give positive and constructive feedback.

- Support consensus decision-making efforts.

- Delegate to team members as much as possible.

Performing

The performing stage of team development is the result of working through the first three stages. By this stage, team members have learned how to work together as a fully functioning team. They can define tasks, work out relationships, manage their conflicts, and work toward accomplishing their mission.

This stage is the most harmonious of all the stages that the team must work through. Team members begin to define what it means to be a part of a fully functioning team

The team makes decisions, diagnoses and solves problems, and takes action. Communication is open and supportive and team members act in concert with each other without fear of rejection.

Leadership is now participative and shared. Different viewpoints and information can be shared openly, and conflict is recognized as the catalyst that generates creativity in the problem-solving process.

A sense of identity

The team now has a sense of its own identity, and team members are committed to the team and its goals. Facilitators can guide the team through this stage by using the following guidelines:

- Observe the team and offer feedback when requested.

- Support new ideas and ways for achieving outcomes.

- Encourage ongoing self-assessment.

- Develop team members to their fullest potential.

- Look for ways to increase the team's capacity.

The Process Is Sequential

As in any developmental process, the stages teams go through have their strong points and weaknesses. The linear progression of team development as described is not always sequential. Facilitators must recognize that the stages of team development—forming, storming, norming, and performing—are well established aspects of the team process, which require close attention to avoid increased frustration and anxiety as the team develops through each stage.

It is important to remember that any change in the composition of the team or its leadership requires returning to the forming stage. In addition, not paying attention to the needed activities in any one stage will cause a return to that stage.

Theories of Group Development

The Tuckman Model[1] (forming, storming, norming, and performing) is generally accepted as the basic model of team development. It incorporates many aspects of the theories considered in this discussion, and has remained relatively constant since it was introduced.

Theorists	Stage 1	Stage 2	Stage 3	Stage 4
Bennis Sheppard	Dependence	Counter-Dependence	Resolution	Inter-dependence
Gibb	Acceptance	Data Flow	Goals and Norms	Control
Schutz	Inclusion	Control	Openness	Deinclusion
Tuckman	Forming	Storming	Norming	Performing
Kormanski Mozenter	Awareness	Conflict	Cooperation	Productivity
Varney	Formation	Building	Working	Maturity

1. *Team Building* by Reddy, W. and Jamison, K. 1988. San Diego, CA: NTL and University Associates.

Team Member Roles

When individuals come together to form a team, a number of dynamics occur simultaneously. Some team members are very goal oriented, while others spend time working on interpersonal issues. Team members often test issues that concern them, such as influence, expertise, conflict management, decision making, and roles. Such tests are part of effective team development.

One aspect of team dynamics is the way in which team members work together to reach their goals. As team development progresses, members settle into individual "roles" by mutual consent. Such roles include both *task* and *process* aspects of the team's interactions.

The member-role viewpoint of team building suggests that the team requires the participation of members in both *task* and *process* areas if it is to develop into a fully functioning team.

For teams to maximize their performance, it is important that each team member understand and play the appropriate role at the right time. Building an effective team is dependent on how the relationships between the dynamics of task and process are managed.

Task Dynamic and Task Roles

The task dynamic is identified by the "what" and "why" issues of the team's work. Task roles within this dynamic include establishing the mission, operating principles, goals, and team member roles. The accomplishment of these tasks drives the team toward its work related objectives.

Some task roles played by team members are as follows:

Information giver	Offers authoritative information or data.
Information seeker	Asks for clarification or accuracy of statements.
Initiator	Makes suggestions or proposes new ideas.
Opinion giver	States belief or opinions relative to the discussion.
Elaborator	Elaborates on ideas and suggestions.
Consensus seeker	Polls the group for its readiness to make decisions or resolve conflicts.
Clarifier	Interprets or explains facts or opinions.
Standard setter	Establishes criteria for evaluating opinions, ideas, or decisions.
Representative	Reports the team's progress or actions outside the team.

No one team member has to perform every task role. Different members can play different roles, and any one individual can play several roles at different times during team activities.

Because teams in their initial stages of development are primarily task oriented, the roles team members play, e.g., opinion giver and information giver, can cause the team to produce lower output. The development of the team is limited unless it can move beyond the initial task role phase of the team.

A task-dominated team focuses primarily on the team's mission, neglecting the process factors. Team members compete with each other at the expense of working together in a collaborative manner. This type of behavior can result in anger, resentment, and alienation—all of which leads to poor morale and frustration. If the team fails to manage the process aspects of the team's dynamics during the early stages of team development, the team will not be successful.

The Process Dynamic and Process Roles

The process dynamic refers to the personal and social needs of team members that contribute to a sense of team cohesiveness. It is the "how" dynamic that the team uses to facilitate task accomplishment.

In comparison to task roles, process roles focus on the team's needs concerning commitment, dependence, and involvement. Team needs are more emotional in nature and relate to self-esteem and the needs of individual egos.

The process dynamic includes such factors as which team members talk, how much they talk, and who talks to whom. This area of team development receives little attention, but it is an area that has the potential to create team problems.

Building a true sense of teamwork requires managing the team's process dynamic. Some process roles, like task roles, can hinder or facilitate the team's interaction. Fortunately, role behaviors that facilitate team dynamics can be learned and effectively practiced in teams. Similarly, the negative behaviors can be minimized using the same learning process.

Some process role qualities displayed by team players are:

Encouraging	Being open to others' opinions or feelings even if they are different.
Gatekeeping	Openly taking interest in what others say, and facilitating communication.
Listening	Paying close attention to what others talk about.
Harmonizing	Negotiating or relieving tension when appropriate.
Yielding	Giving up an unpopular viewpoint and admitting mistakes.
Accepting	Respecting and promoting differences.
Supporting	Giving team members permission to feel good about their successes.

Task and Process Involvement

Team members need to feel that they are part of the team's activities. They rely on one another and share responsibilities in order to get the job done. Involvement is the most important incentive that fosters effective team work.

When team members feel committed and feel like their teammates are equally committed, a sense of interdependence develops. They recognize that accomplishment of the team's mission will only happen if the team pulls together rather than working individually.

A process-dominated team places emphasis on interpersonal relationships at the expense of resolving disagreements and conflict. The team will have difficulty achieving the designated task, but will feel good about working together because they are involved and committed to each other.

As demonstrated below, task roles have a tendency to dominate during the early stages of the team's development; whereas, process roles increase in their importance during the later teambuilding stages.

As the team matures, task and process roles parallel each other in their importance, which contributes to the effective functioning of the team. Individual contribution subordinates itself to team effort.

The team must acquire a balance of task and process functions if it is to realize its potential as a fully functioning team.

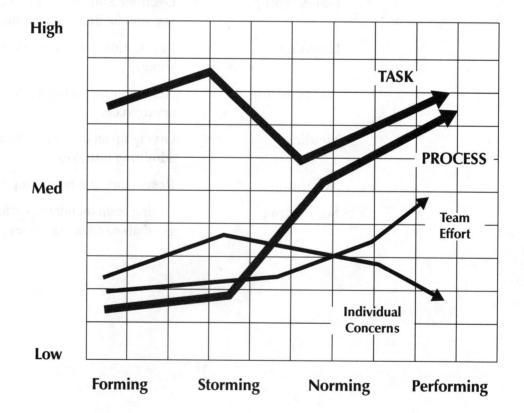

Dysfunctional Team Member Behaviors

Dysfunctional team member behaviors can impact the work flow of the team if not appropriately challenged. Some task behaviors can interfere with the team's accomplishing its goal.

Similarly, some process behaviors can prevent the team from developing a supportive team climate.

Some of the dysfunctional task behaviors are as follows:

Condescending	Putting down team member contributions as irrelevant.
Bullying	Being inconsiderate of other team member's needs.
Blocking	Arguing too much on a point and rejecting expressed ideas without consideration.
Avoiding	Not paying attention to facts or relevant ideas.
Withdrawing	Acting passive or indifferent, wandering from the subject of discussion.
Joking	Excessive playing around, telling jokes, and mimicking other members.
Dominating	Excessive talking, interrupting others, criticizing, and blaming.
Self-Seeking	Putting one's personal needs before the team's needs.

If team members exhibit dysfunctional task behaviors, the team leader or team members must respond immediately.

Responsive Actions

Some response actions are as follows:

- **Provide individual counseling.**

  A member of the team should meet with the disruptive team member in a one-on-one session. During the meeting, it is important to deliver specific feedback about the behavior or behaviors in question and the consequences if the behaviors continue.

- **Confront the individual.**

  If individual counseling does not work, the team may decide to confront the disruptive behavior during a team meeting. This strategy is excellent because it can provide immediate feedback on the behaviors in question. In addition, the team members can offer support.

- **Ask the member to leave.**

  If all else fails, the team has the right to ask the disruptive team member to leave the team. This is quite a challenge for the team as a whole because it requires team members to work in concert solving problems and making decisions. Although it is uncommon to terminate a member involuntarily, such situations do occur.

  It is important that all team members understand why the member is being asked to leave and participate in the decision process.

Successful teams have members who play a variety of task and process roles. The greater understanding that members have of these roles and their consequences, the better equipped the team is to accomplish overall team goals.

Team Communication

Team communication is defined as the exchange of information between team members that is satisfactorily transmitted, received and acted upon. Communication includes the transference and understanding of meaning between the sender and the receiver. An idea, regardless of its value, is just an idea until other team members understand it. The quality of the team's work, to a large extent, depends on the quality of information they share.

The Process of Communication

All communication originates when one person who wants to convey information to another person. Information includes such things as facts, feelings, values, and opinions. The person who originates the communication is called the sender. To transfer information to another person, the sender must first translate the thoughts into symbols that will be recognized and understood. This process is called encoding the message.

When the message has been encoded, the next part of the process is to communicate the message to the receiver. This can be done in many ways such as face-to-face, electronic media, or printed material.

Once the message is received by another person, the decoding process begins. Similar to how the sender must translate thoughts into symbols that will be recognized, the receiver must interpret the symbols by decoding the information in ways that provide meaning for the receiver. If the receiver translates the sender's message as it was conveyed by the sender, effective communication occurs. If not, ineffective communication results.

Unfortunately, not all people have the same types of experiences, which would ensure effective encoding and decoding of transferable messages. People attach different meanings to words, sounds, and nonverbal gestures as they attempt to communicate and to understand what is being communicated.

Communication problems develop when team members do not share a common language or understand the difference between facts, feelings, values, and opinions.

The Process of Communication

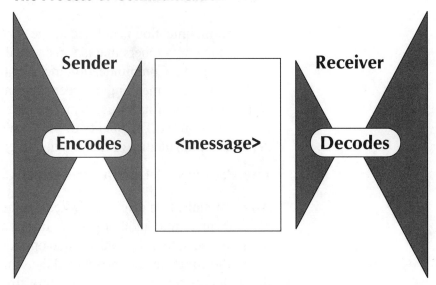

Speaking a Common Language

The team's language often reflects the state of the team's development; whether they are in the forming, storming, norming, or performing stage. In addition, a task-oriented team discusses issues such as mission, goals, time schedules, and quality measures. Whereas a process-oriented team discusses feelings, values, cooperation, and focus. Although the two languages are related in their purpose, the mismatch of process and task language is typically responsible for causing team member miscommunication, among other variables.

The ability of team members to understand and communicate information in both the task and process dynamics enables team members to better understand and work together.

Task Communication

TASK COMMUNICATION

Task communication is usually introduced by the statement, "I think that . . ."

Task communication is:

- Analytical.

- Linear.

- Explicit.

- Verbal.

- Auditory.

- Concrete.

- Active.

Talking from the head

Task communication is "head talk" that leads to the explanation of the team situation. It is bound by rules of logic that may or may not be true. A task statement can be proven or disproven. Words must be communicated in order to produce task statements.

The statement, "I think that . . ." is indicative of the speaker using "task" communication. Task communication is analytical, linear, explicit, verbal, auditory, concrete, active, and adaptive.

Some task statements that team members make are:

- "Our purpose is solely to achieve the mission."

- "We have to take some kind of action immediately."

- "Emotions have nothing to do with our work."

Process Communication

+---+
| ### PROCESS COMMUNICATION |
| |
| Process communication is usually introduced by |
| the statement, "I feel . . ." |
| |
| Process communication is: |
| |
| • Intuitive. |
| |
| • Spontaneous. |
| |
| • Emotional. |
| |
| • Visual. |
| |
| • Artistic. |
| |
| • Playful. |
+---+

**Talking from
the heart**

Process communication is "gut" talk that leads to an understanding of the team situation. It explains an individual's internal, affective, nonrational response. Process statements are usually personal in nature and refer to the individual's state of being. They are neither good or bad, nor true or false.

In North America, denial of feelings is so customary that many people resort to intellectualizing their thoughts in order to conceal their feelings. Some common statements made in tense discussions are "Now, let's not get personal," or "Let's just stick to the work and not let our feelings interfere with it."

When process statements are made, the form is usually stated as "I feel . . ." (adjective) or "I feel . . ." (adverb). Process communication is intuitive, spontaneous, emotional, visual, artistic, playful, and innovative.

Some process statements that team members make are:

• "Our ability to collaborate together makes me feel good."

• "The more we share information the easier it is to work."

• "Synergy is the outcome of our team process."

Effective Team Communication

Effective communication results when team members take responsibility for their thoughts, feelings, and overt behaviors. Team members who own their thoughts and feelings and communicate using both task and process communication will have a greater influence on the team and ultimately on the team's mission.

Barriers to Effective Team Communication

Barriers in team communication result from the inability of team members to distinguish the various communication channels in which we speak, such as facts, individual feelings, personal values, and opinions. When two or more people are in discussion, any one of the preceding communication channels can cause distortion and communication breakdown if it is not clearly understood and responded to in a congruent manner.

Facts	A fact is something that has actually happened or that is really true without any emotional reference.
Feelings	Feelings refer to any subjective reaction, pleasurable or unpleasurable, that a person may have to a situation, sometimes with the absence of reason.
Values	Values refer to important personal ideals that make people behave the way they do.
Opinions	Opinions are a set of beliefs not based on absolute certainty but on what seems true to one's own mind.

Usually one or all of the above are involved in any type of team communication. For example, when a team first comes together much of the communication is related to the task of the team and facts usually predominate. Feelings are involved to the extent that team members collaborate and work together sharing their experiences. Values come into play almost immediately as individuals discuss what is important to them in their interactions.

Finally, opinions shift continually to new information and influences in the team's process.

Barriers to effective communication occur when there is a lack of clarity or a mismatch of communication channels. The most frequent mismatch in the communication process occurs when team members mix fact and opinion.

Interpreting Facts and Opinions

Team members miscommunicate when they misinterpret facts from opinions. A team member, for example, will discuss team issues stating only his or her opinion about a particular issue such as, "You don't understand the concept." Unfortunately, the listener may hear the opinion as fact, i.e., something that is true rather than hearing the response as just the sender's opinion. The listener may react from the feeling level with a response such as, "You're not qualified to make a judgment on whether I understand it or not."

From outward appearance, the original statement seems to be factual but carries with it some feelings toward the listener.

The statement may be true or not. However, the response from the listener is usually anger or frustration which immediately interferes with the communication process. This eventually leads to further communication breakdown.

A basic notion about communication channels is that unrecognized communication that conveys values, feelings, and opinions under the guise of facts applies subtle pressures on the listeners. They may feel pressured to agree, conform, or to defend themselves against what may be perceived as hostile feelings.

An awareness of the communication channels and an ability to distinguish between them, will produce greater understanding, empathy, and consideration on both sides of the communication exchange.

Overcoming Communication Barriers

The first step in overcoming communication barriers is to acknowledge and call attention to the four communication channels. This is referred to as making a process statement. For example, a team member might say, "Sharon, you seem to be upset. Let's discuss the situation further before we continue. I want to make sure we understand each other without any hard feelings." This statement acknowledges Sharon's feelings and brings them into a more congruent communication channel that Sharon recognizes. After Sharon's feelings are acknowledged, the conversation can return to the "factual" channel to complete the discussion.

Some phrases, such as "the facts are clear," "I feel," "to me," and "in my opinion" are effective in breaking communication barriers. Such phrases call direct attention to the four communication channels and separate them so that the sender and the receiver in the communication process can manage them separately.

The four communication channels

Understanding and responding to team member communication channels congruently will enhance the team communication process.

Communication Channel	Phrase Response
1. Facts	"The facts are . . ."
2. Feelings	"I feel . . ."
3. Values	"To me . . ."
4. Opinions	"In my opinion . . ."

Giving and Receiving Feedback

BENEFITS OF GIVING FEEDBACK

- Feedback reduces uncertainty.

- Feedback solves problems.

- Feedback builds trust.

- Feedback can strengthen relationships.

- Feedback improves work quality.

Almost all aspects of team communication involve feedback—giving and receiving information about team-related performance. Team members give feedback through various means to team members as well as others in the organization. Smart team members solicit feedback about their own behavior, new ideas, and team procedures. However, despite its inevitability and importance, feedback is an aspect of team membership that few members enjoy or perform effectively.

Why Consider Feedback?

Any time team members give verbal reactions to another's ideas, they are engaged in the process of giving feedback. Even a raised eyebrow or a scowled look constitutes nonverbal feedback. The feedback can be subtle or explicit. Which ever it is, team members must be constantly aware of the feedback process. In addition, team members must become aware of the unintentional displays of feedback and recognize the advantages of developing positive feedback skills.

Benefits of Giving Feedback

By giving clear and concise feedback, team members and the entire organization will benefit. Some benefits of giving feedback are as follows:

1. **Feedback reduces uncertainty.**

   All team members need to know where they stand in job performance. Seldom do they ask, but they always want to know whether their performance measures up.

2. **Feedback solves problems.**

   If there is a performance problem, early feedback can usually solve it before it magnifies into a situation that requires extreme action.

3. **Feedback can build trust.**

   Trust means being comfortable in your interactions with others. You are in a good position to predict other team member's behavior if they are honest with you over time. By directly sharing information, you can reduce suspicions and fears among team members. Team members who regularly give feedback to others are more predictable than those who do not. Other team members know what to expect, appreciate the predictability, and show less defensiveness, and more respect.

4. **Feedback can strengthen relationships.**

   Team members who can be honest in their reactions to others tend to develop stronger interpersonal relationships. While the feedback process can sometimes be trying, the ability to communicate openly leads to a greater commitment in the relationship.

5. **Feedback improves work quality.**

   Team members cannot be expected to improve their work quality unless they have a clear understanding of what is expected of them. In addition, positive feedback for excellent performance creates incentives for improved quality of work.

Giving Feedback to Others

Giving feedback is a verbal or nonverbal process in which a team member shares his or her feelings or perceptions about another team member's behavior or actions.

The process of giving and receiving feedback is one of the most important ways for learning new behaviors and determining the impact of our behavior on others. Some guidelines for giving feedback are as follows:

1. **Feedback should be specific.**

   It is important to give clear examples of the behavior or performance that is being discussed. The greater clarity you have in describing the behavior, the more the other person will understand it.

2. **Be descriptive, not evaluative with feedback.**

   This means that you should describe behavior in observable terms rather than using words that may seem to be judgmental. Referring to observable behavior means dealing in the realm of fact—either a team member interrupts the discussion or not. Using evaluative labels and name calling moves the feedback into the emotional realm and deals with opinions. Mixing fact and opinion often creates communication barriers as discussed previously.

3. **Be timely with the feedback.**

   Feedback is most effective when it is given right after the work performance or behavior occurs. Timing also means giving feedback privately and when there is time for discussion.

4. **Feedback must be on-going.**

   Good feedback should be an on-going experience in team member relationships. If giving feedback becomes a routine part of team communication, the feedback process will greatly enhance overall team effectiveness.

The ways in which people give feedback may be influenced by their values and personal philosophies, about how they relate to others, and about people in general. These guidelines can be learned and are valuable in assisting team members in giving useful feedback.

Receiving Feedback from Others

RECEIVING FEEDBACK FROM OTHERS

- Get as much information as possible.

- Do not become defensive.

- Use the feedback you solicit.

Giving and receiving feedback are two important parts of effective team communication. The guidelines presented will assist team members in developing open channels of communication where team members can learn and grow from each other.

There should be reciprocity in feedback. If team members can give it, they should be able to receive it. When soliciting feedback from others, it is helpful to follow these guidelines:

1. **Get as much information as possible.**

   The more specific the feedback, the more useful it will be. Whether the solicitation is formal or informal, make certain that questions are specific. Sometimes team members will be either vague, or global with their reactions. If this occurs, the person asking for feedback must probe for the details in order to make the information useful. If the outcome of the feedback is to make changes, it must be specific so that you know what to change.

2. **Do not become defensive.**

   One of the tendencies that occurs when receiving feedback is to become defensive. It is important to listen to what is being communicated and to avoid the motorboat syndrome— "yes, but . . . but . . . but . . . but!" We often want to deny the feedback and immediately provide refutation. For feedback to be useful, team members must avoid defensive responses.

3. **Use the feedback you solicit.**

   The feedback we receive from others is often valid. Feedback should be welcomed. It is important to study it and use it to make changes in behavior if you feel it is necessary. Not all feedback comments, however, should be accepted without close consideration to the information and the person giving the feedback. Often, feedback may say more about the person giving the feedback then it does about the person receiving it.

   Nevertheless, successful team members appreciate others' feedback and use it to make improvements in their behavior when appropriate.

Making Decisions

Decision making is a process by which team members arrive at a decision, judgment, or conclusion through a process of deliberation. It is one of the most critical applications for effective teamwork. Consider your own team situation. How much time is spent during team meetings actually making decisions?

The Difference Between Making Decisions and Solving Problems

Decision making and problem solving are two different types of team processes that require two very different methods for accomplishing their outcomes.

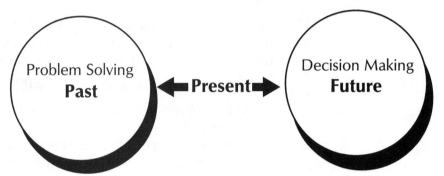

Problem Solving	Problem solving has its origins in the past. A problem is something that has gone wrong in the past and must be managed in the present. It is more precise and objective than decision making.
Decision Making	Decision making is rooted in the present with a look into the future for resolution. A decision is a commitment to a course of action selected from several alternatives.

When determining whether to make decisions or solve problems, try to answer the following questions:

- Is the issue related to past circumstances? If the answer is yes, ask the second question. Do we know why something went wrong? If the answer is no, start the problem-solving process.

- Is the issue related to past circumstances? If the answer is no, start the decision-making process giving consideration to different types of decisions that can be made.

Types of Decisions

When considering possible courses of action, team members must evaluate the objectives, alternatives, and potential risks of their decision. Decisions can be classified into four different categories:

1. **Complex decisions.**

   Complex decisions require large amounts of information and involvement by all team members.

2. **Yes-and-no decisions.**

   Yes-and-no decisions involve two alternatives—either to accept or reject the proposal.

3. **Single-course-of-action decisions.**

   Single-course-of-action decisions involve determining whether the proposed measure should be implemented.

4. **One-alternative decisions.**

   One-alternative decisions are concerned with whether a measure should be adopted.

When dealing with the types of decisions described above, it is important to have a rational decision-making process in place so that all team members can join in making the decision when needed.

Implementing Decisions

Some teams make many decisions that are never implemented. Therefore, it is important to include an implementation strategy when any type of decision is made. Without this strategy, follow-through is less likely to occur. The strategy can be as specific as developing a step-by-step action plan or as general as assigning the implementation of the decision to another team member. In any case, the implementation of any decision requires accountability.

Successful teams develop a successful decision-making process. Without this ability, teams will never move beyond the discussion of problems.

A Decision-Making Procedure

When the team is ready to make a decision, it is important that team members understand what decision must be made and how the decision will be made. To clarify the decision-making process, follow the steps below:

1. **Clarify the purpose.**

   A decision-making process must begin with a clear understanding of the factors surrounding the decision to be made.

2. **Establish criteria by considering the results the team wants.**

   The criteria represent the basis on which the team will actually decide. In a team situation, the team leader should make certain that the team members who are going to be influenced by the decision have the opportunity to provide input.

3. **Separate the criteria by classifying them into two categories—limiting factors and desirable features.**

   Limiting factors include criteria such as the budget and time restrictions that any option must meet.

   Desirable features should be listed according to their priority and include items such as location and access.

4. **Generate options by weighing the limiting factors of each of the desirable options.**

   Make a list of the acceptable options.

5. **Compare options.**

   Collect data on each option. This will help the team to measure the satisfaction on each criterion.

6. **Identify the risks of each option.**

   Do each one separately and determine the concerns that the team has about the ultimate effects of each option.

7. **Assess the risks of each option by ranking them.**

   Rank each of the options according to probability (that is, on a scale of 10 to 1, where 10 = likely and 1 = unlikely).

8. **Make the decision.**

   The team should make a decision using one of the following procedures: decision by authority, decision by minority, the democratic process (majority rule), consensus, or unanimity. The consensus decision-making process and unanimity achieve the greatest buy-in from team members. However, both require time, an all important resource, to achieve.

Decision-Making Methods

The methods that facilitate team decision making are as follows:

1. **Decision by authority.**

   Decision by authority occurs when the highest ranking authority within the team, usually the appointed team leader or manager, makes a unilateral decision. This method is appropriate when the manager or team leader is totally accountable for the team's final decision. Unless there is complete trust in the leader, unilateral decision-making can create conflict among team members if they are not part of the decision process.

2. **Decision by minority.**

   Decision by minority occurs when a small group of team members exert their influence over the majority of the team. This decision-making method is appropriate when the minority members have either expert knowledge or strong feelings about the issue. However, this method can create resentment and hostility among team members if a strong-willed and vocal minority "railroads" decisions that the majority of the group opposes.

3. **The democratic process.**

   The democratic process of decision making occurs when a majority of team members agrees with the issues. This method is the most popular because it is based on democratic principles. It is the principle that a majority, constituted by 50 percent plus 1, will have the power to make decisions binding for the entire team. It is an appropriate procedure when time is limited and when the consequences of the decision will not have a negative impact on the team members in the minority who are not voting in favor of the decision.

4. **Decision by consensus.**

   Decision by consensus means finding a proposal that is acceptable to all team members. For a team to use the consensus decision-making process, there must be sufficient time to make a decision, a creative climate to support the process, and active participation by all team members who have mutual trust, respect, and a commitment to work through the process.

5. **Decision by unanimity.**

   Decision by unanimity occurs when all team members are in full agreement with the decision. This procedure is often confused with consensus decision making. The team should make unanimous decisions when the team issues are important and effect all team members.

Solving Problems

One of the primary responsibilities of team membership is the ability to solve problems that impact the team. To be effective, team members must be able to identify problems and have a desire to resolve them. Trying to solve a problem without a systematic process is like trying to find your way in the wilderness without a good topographical map.

Problem-Solving Steps

The first thing team members must do is to identify the problem to be resolved. Once the problem is identified, the team can work toward solving it. The following considerations will assist a team in finding solutions to team problems.

1. **Define the problem.**

    In this first step, it is important that team members clearly identify the problem that they want to resolve. Working on an ill defined problem can be a waste of time and team resources.

    Some questions that will help define the problem are as follows:

    - What is the actual problem?
    - Is there more than one problem in the initial problem statement?
    - What is the impact of the problem on the team?
    - What impact does the team have on the problem?
    - Who else is affected by the problem and in what way?
    - Has anyone tried to solve the problem before?
    - Why weren't the previous attempts more successful?
    - What did work?

2. **Identify the desired future state.**

    In this second step, it is important that team members describe the outcome or the situation as they would like to see it. If the team's statement of the desired future state can be identified by both quantitative and qualitative information, it will be easier to reach the goal.

3. **Identify forces driving toward change and forces restraining change.**

   Once the desired future state has been defined, the forces that are working for change (driving forces) and those working against change (restraining forces) must be identified. One method is to list all forces that might influence the targeted change.

4. **Analyze forces that can be changed.**

   Once the targeted change and the driving and restraining forces have been identified, consider which forces are more easily changeable. Change occurs in two ways: (1) increase the strength of the current driving forces or add new ones or (2) reduce the strength of the restraining forces or eliminate them all together.

5. **Plan a strategy for change.**

   In this step, the team must work on developing strategies to solve the problem. There may be movement slightly between driving and restraining forces but the situation is a delicate balance between finding the right variables to exert force upon.

6. **Develop an action plan.**

   In step six, the team must design an action plan that will affect the forces working either for or against the problem resolution. The plan should include identifying team members who will be accountable for following through with the problem-solving solutions.

7. **Implement the plan.**

   Put your plan into action!

8. **Evaluate.**

   In this final step, team members must evaluate the effectiveness of their plan. The objective of this step is to determine if the plan has achieved the desired team outcome. If the team's actions did not produce the desired results, they should be reevaluated so that other actions can be considered.

Making the Problem-Solving Process Work

The problem-solving process discussed above is only as good as the team that attempts to use it. An effective problem-solving team must be made up of individuals who feel free to express their ideas and opinions in an atmosphere of openness, sharing, and trust.

Managing Team Conflict

Conflict is a daily reality for all team members. Team members' needs and values inevitably come into conflict with the needs and values of others. Some of the conflicts are minor and can be managed easily while others have a greater intensity and require a strategy for effective resolution. The ability to resolve team conflict is the most important skill that team members can develop.

Causes of Team Conflict

To gain better understanding of the causes of conflict, we will examine five perspectives that contribute to conflict situations.

Personality

Personality differences contribute the most to creating conflict situations in team settings. Such differences can be as simple as whether members are introverted or extroverted, make decisions based on facts and logic or intuition and feelings, or whether members are spontaneous or planners in how they organize their environment.

Values

Team members often express different points of view based on a set of values carried with them into any team situation. When team members discuss the work of the team, their values act as driving forces that control their responses and interactions. For example, if one team member believes in working through a difficult situation in a collaborative manner (value = working collaboratively) and the other believes that competition is the only way to respond (value = competition), team members will have a hard time managing their differences based on the values they bring into the situation.

Perspective

Team members have different ways of seeing and experiencing the world. Although differences in team member perspectives can be a positive attribute for the team, the differences in perspective can be the cause of conflict on the team.

Goals

Some team members have personal agendas that may be different from team goals. These are called "hidden agendas" or undisclosed individual outcomes. Such agendas may be achieved at the expense of other team members.

Culture

Since many teams are made up of individuals from diverse backgrounds, different cultural attitudes, values, and beliefs may cause conflict within the team. The inability of team members to understand different world views and appreciate the richness that diversity brings to the team contributes to team conflict.

Conflict Management Strategies

Conflict occurs when the needs, wants, or values of team members clash. As a result, team members may react to the conflict in five basic ways: They either compete, collaborate, avoid, accommodate or compromise with one another.

1. **Competition.**

   Competition is characterized by the need to win at all costs. It is a win-lose situation with the need to dominate.

2. **Collaboration.**

   Collaboration is characterized by a desire to satisfy all team members in a win-win situation.

3. **Avoidance.**

   Avoidance is characterized by attempts to distract attention from the issue or ignore it completely.

4. **Accommodation.**

   Accommodation is characterized by the desire to please others at the expense of a person's own needs.

5. **Compromise.**

   Compromise is described by meeting the conflict at midpoint. Both parties in a dispute achieve moderate but incomplete satisfaction.

When to Use Conflict Strategies

Using the appropriate conflict strategy is important when managing conflict situations. Try to discern which conflict resolution approach can be used most effectively for a given situation.

Conflict is useful when it helps stimulate creativity and innovation and provides the medium through which problems can be discussed and tensions released. Evidence suggests conflict can improve the quality of decision making by allowing different points of view to be examined.

Conflict is an antidote for "group think." It does not allow the team to passively accept decisions that may be based on incomplete or inappropriate information. It challenges the status quo and facilitates the consideration of new ideas.

CONFLICT RESOLUTION: COMPETITION

Competition is appropriate when:

- Quick, decisive action is necessary.
- The issues are important and unpopular actions need to be implemented.
- The issues are vital to the team's welfare and you know you are right.
- When dealing with people who take advantage of non-competitive behavior.
- Other options are not possible.

CONFLICT RESOLUTION: COLLABORATION

Collaboration is appropriate when:

- You need to find an integrative solution and both sets of concerns are too important to be compromised.
- Your objective is to learn.
- You need to merge insights from people with different perspectives.
- You want to gain commitment by incorporating concerns into a consensus decision.
- You want to work through feelings that have interfered with a relationship.

CONFLICT RESOLUTION: AVOIDANCE

Avoidance is appropriate when:

- An issue is trivial or more important issues are pressing.
- You see that there is no chance to satisfy your major concerns.
- You need to let people cool down and regain perspective.
- You need more time to gather information.
- Others can resolve the conflict more effectively.

CONFLICT RESOLUTION: ACCOMMODATION

Accommodation is appropriate when:

- You find that you are wrong.
- You want to show your reasonableness.
- Issues are more important to others than yourself.
- You want to build social support for later use.
- You want to minimize your losses.
- You want to allow other team members to develop by learning from mistakes.

CONFLICT RESOLUTION: COMPROMISE

Compromise is appropriate when:

- Goals are important but not worth the effort of disruption.
- Opponents with equal power are committed to different means to a similar end.
- You want to achieve temporary settlements to complex issues.
- You want to strive at an expedient solution under time pressure.
- You need backup because collaboration or competition is not working.

Self-Authorized Team Leadership

The principles of traditional models of leadership are power, authority, and subordinate control. These leadership principles that were once effective now hinder team members' ability to adapt to rapidly changing work environments. Today, by contrast, organizations need team members who can capitalize on their own ability to be self-authorized team leaders.

Self-authorized team leadership is a form of "accountable followership" in which team members assume responsibility for their performance and their relationships with other team members. Self-authorized leadership is based on four assumptions:

- All team members practice some degree of self-authorized leadership.

- Self-authorized leadership is applicable to all team members.

- Not all team members are effective self-authorized leaders.

- Self-authorized leadership can be developed.

Behavioral and cognitive strategies

To be successful, self-authorized leaders employ two types of strategies that serve to direct their development and performance: behavioral strategies and cognitive strategies.

Behavioral Strategies

BEHAVIORAL STRATEGIES

- Self-imposed outcomes.

- Self-management of workplace behaviors.

- Self-observations of outcomes.

- Self-rewards.

Behavioral strategies are self-directed action efforts that direct team member performance to excellence. The strategies are as follows:

- **Self-imposed outcomes.**

    Self-imposed outcomes help establish direction and priorities. They are the most important component of self-authorized leadership; they focus on personal growth and professional development.   Self-imposed outcomes must be clear, challenging, and attainable.

- **Self-management of workplace behaviors.**

    Self-management of workplace behaviors helps model appropriate methods of interaction between team members. Behaviors can be preferred and supported or unwanted and inhibited.

- **Self-observation of outcomes.**

    Self-observation of outcomes focuses on the consequences of completed tasks. Observations of what worked and what didn't work are helpful in determining future efforts.

- **Self-rewards.**

    Self-rewards are important reinforcers for preferred behaviors. They can be both physical or psychological; they serve to reward effort and maintain high levels of motivation.

Cognitive Strategies

COGNITIVE STRATEGIES

- Self-knowledge.
- Skill.
- Self-control.
- Purpose.

Cognitive strategies focus on the naturally rewarding aspects of teamwork. Four strategies that promote a positive attitude toward teamwork are as follows:

- **Self-knowledge.**

  Knowing that you have an awareness and understanding of the range of information you need to do your job.

- **Skill.**

  Knowing that you have the expertness that comes from training and practice.

- **Self-control.**

  Knowing that you have some control over what happens on the job.

- **Purpose.**

  Knowing that your work is meaningful, with a specific end in view.

Increasing Leadership Effectiveness

INCREASING LEADERSHIP EFFECTIVENESS

- Maintaining an outcome orientation.

- Focusing attention.

- Leading others by example.

- Balancing the mind and heart.

Self-authorized team leaders who want to increase their effectiveness as team members can do so by using the following strategies: maintaining an outcome orientation, focusing attention, leading others by example, and balancing the mind and heart.

Maintaining an outcome orientation

Maintaining an outcome orientation allows self-authorized team leaders to see their experiences as a set of choices. Rather than addressing the issue of "why" a problem exists, it organizes experience around "what" is wanted and "how" it becomes possible to achieve it. When a specific outcome is decided upon, it becomes possible to turn those examples of not getting what you want into valuable feedback. You no longer fail at your endeavors but learn from your experiences.

Focusing attention

Focusing attention refers to the ability to have a clear set of goals and priorities that result from maintaining an outcome orientation. A person who is able to focus attention knows where they are going and doesn't waste precious time getting there.

Leading others by example

Leading others by example is the "golden rule" of self-authorized team leadership. It refers to modeling appropriate behaviors such as respecting, supporting, listening, communicating, collaborating, and being sensitive to the needs of all team members.

Balancing the heart and mind

Balancing the heart and mind allows self-authorized team leaders to engage both the subjective and analytical thinking processes of the mind. The goal is to create a balance, or alignment, between how we feel and think, which is necessary if we are going to be working effectively with other team members.

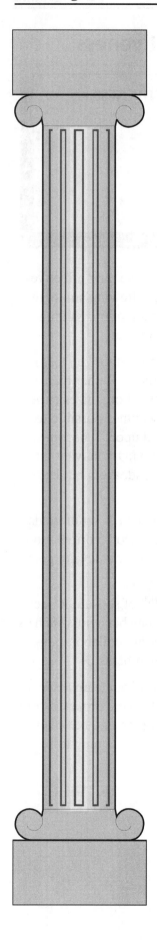

The Seven Pillars of Leadership Character

An effective approach to empowering self-authorized team leaders is the adherence to the seven pillars of leadership character. The seven pillars are values that serve as a foundation for effective self-authorized team leadership. The seven pillars that form the foundation are caring, courage, honesty, integrity, responsibility, loyalty, and fairness.

Caring The ability to show others that you care about them through kindness, generosity, sharing, and compassion.

Courage The attitude or response of facing and dealing with anything recognized as dangerous, difficult, or painful, instead of withdrawing from it.

Honesty The willingness to be truthful and sincere without deceiving or misleading others or withholding important information in relationships of trust.

Integrity The ability to stand up for your own beliefs about right and wrong and show commitment, courage, and self-discipline in everyday team member interactions.

Responsibility The ability to think before you act, giving consideration to the possible consequences of your interactions as well as exercising self-control and self-discipline.

Loyalty The willingness to stand by and support other team members without talking behind people's backs, spreading rumors, or engaging in harmful gossip.

Fairness The ability to treat all team members alike without prejudgment and to make decisions only on appropriate considerations.

Self-authorized team leadership is a concept that places the responsibility of leadership on the shoulders of each team member. As team members assume responsibility for their actions and relationships with others, they share leadership responsibilities in all aspects of the team's work.

Chapter Three:

Planning the Workshop

This chapter contains general suggestions and comments to assist you with planning the teambuilding workshops.

Four important tasks in beginning are as follows:

- Read through this book.

- Define your particular needs for teambuilding training.

- Adjust the material to fit your needs.

- Prepare the session.

CHAPTER OVERVIEW

This chapter contains general tips on how to prepare for your supervision workshop, including:

- Managing your own training program.
- Getting ready.
- Presentation checklist.
- Facilitator preparation.
- Conducting the workshop.
- Workshop follow-up.

Define Your Training Needs

This task is essentially a needs assessment that can be either as simple and informal or as complex and formal as you desire. We are not going to discuss the "ins and outs" of conducting needs assessment, but will simply observe that there are a number of sources which you can draw upon to gather the information that you need. Some of these sources include:

- Your own knowledge and awareness of the teambuilding situation in your organization.

- The team population.

- The specific needs of each team member.

- Overall outcomes desired from teambuilding efforts.

Having gathered the information you require, you are ready to move forward and develop a training session to meet your particular needs.

Adjusting Materials to Fit

The cover of this book says, "customizable designs." So, let's talk about how you can customize these materials to fit your own needs.

You need to do a minimum amount of personal customization to assure that you cover all relevant issues.

In addition, you will need to pay attention to the session timing to fit the needs and schedules of your team members. Beyond that, you have complete freedom to do as much or as little customization as you wish.

Integrating Your Own Materials

A good way to ensure a high level of relevance in this training is to select specific training materials that you currently use and then integrate them into these sessions where appropriate.

- Use your materials with those provided here.

- Substitute your materials.

- Blend your materials to create an enhanced presentation.

Workshop Agenda Template

Use this generic workshop agenda template to outline your programs and plan what methods and media to use.

Agenda	Topics, Key Points	Time Allotted	Start	Stop	Training Method	Media	Sourcebook Pages
1. Start-up	• Welcome • Housekeeping						
2. Agenda	• Schedule • Key topics • Objectives						
3. Introductions							
4. Thought-starter							
5. Core material							
6. Break							
7. Core material							
8. Lunch							
9. Thought-starter							
10. Core material							
11. Break							
12. Core material							
13. Evaluations							
14. Adjourn							

Getting Ready

You are now ready to establish the agenda for your teambuilding training sessions. You know what you want to emphasize and what information you might add or delete.

Organizing the Sessions

At this point, you are ready to transition into the logistics of getting ready. However, there are a few things that must be addressed before you begin.

Here are some tasks that you might want to consider which might be relevant to your situation.

• Negotiate the number of participants, number of sessions, and time to be allocated to training.

• Establish a procedure for announcing the sessions.

• Prepare materials such as announcements, pre-workshop preparation packages, invitation letters, enrollment, etc.

If you have a well defined method for doing the above, the job should be relatively simple. If not, it will require more effort in the beginning. You will find a basic level of assistance in the remainder of this chapter.

Workshop Checklist

Program title: _____

Program date: _____ Time: _____

Name of facilitator: _____

Location: _____

Number of participants: _____

Administration Issues

☐ Schedule meeting site

☐ Determine furniture arrangement

☐ Determine food and beverage service

☐ Determine access time and method

☐ Distribute workshop announcements

☐ Send participant confirmations

Participant Materials

☐ Name tags or tent cards

☐ Handouts

☐ Copies of facilitator's biographical sketch (1 page)

☐ Pens or pencils

☐ Ruled paper

☐ Evaluations

☐ Hard candy or mints

☐ Prizes (optional)

Trainer Materials

☐ Workshop agenda

☐ Training plan

☐ Overhead transparencies

☐ Videos/Films

☐ 2' by 3' chart pads

☐ Hand-lettered charts

☐ Felt-tip markers

☐ Transparency pens

☐ Masking tape

☐ Cellophane tape

☐ Dry-erase markers

☐ Chalk

☐ Erasers

☐ Three-hole punch

☐ Staples

☐ Staple puller

Master Checklist

Task	By Whom?	When?
Agenda		
☐ Session dates and times	_____	_____
☐ Delete events that you will exclude	_____	_____
☐ Add new events	_____	_____
☐ Adjust times	_____	_____
☐ Identify breaks and stop times	_____	_____
☐ Add "start" and "stop" times	_____	_____
Facilities ☐ Date arrangements must be completed	_____	_____
☐ Enter requirements information	_____	_____
☐ Date/Time of session	_____	_____
☐ Number of participants	_____	_____
☐ Number of additional rooms	_____	_____
Enrollment ☐ Key dates for enrollment activities	_____	_____
☐ Draft session announcements	_____	_____
☐ Draft enrollment acknowledgments	_____	_____
Duplicate material ☐ Date required: _____	_____	_____
☐ Other special requirements	_____	_____
☐ Delete items not used	_____	_____
☐ Additional materials not listed	_____	_____
Overheads ☐ Date required: _____	_____	_____
☐ Delete transparencies not needed	_____	_____
☐ Additional transparencies not listed	_____	_____
Flipcharts ☐ Date required: _____	_____	_____
☐ Delete flipcharts not used	_____	_____
☐ Additional flipcharts not listed	_____	_____
Catering ☐ Date required: _____	_____	_____
	_____	
Other	_____	

Participant Roster

Workshop Title: _____

Trainer(s): _____

Date: _____   **Time:** _____

Location: _____

_____

	Participant Name	Extension	Department
1.	_____	_____	_____
2.	_____	_____	_____
3.	_____	_____	_____
4.	_____	_____	_____
5.	_____	_____	_____
6.	_____	_____	_____
7.	_____	_____	_____
8.	_____	_____	_____
9.	_____	_____	_____
10.	_____	_____	_____
11.	_____	_____	_____
12.	_____	_____	_____
13.	_____	_____	_____
14.	_____	_____	_____
15.	_____	_____	_____
16.	_____	_____	_____
17.	_____	_____	_____
18.	_____	_____	_____
19.	_____	_____	_____
20.	_____	_____	_____

Facilities and Furniture

Room setup depends on the group's size and room's physical characteristics. Three possible configurations are:

1. **U-shape.**

   The U-shape is recommended for ten to twenty people. Avoid seating people on the inside of the U.

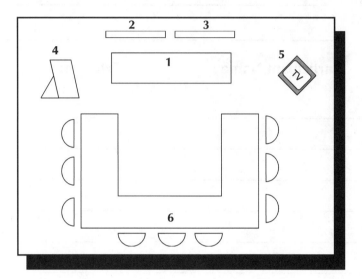

2. **Angled rows.**

   Suitable for groups of twenty or more. Arrange rectangular tables seating two or three people in a chevron pattern. Leave aisles that are wide enough for you to move about the room comfortably.

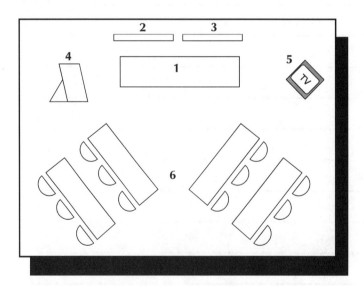

3. Round tables.

Round tables that seat four to five people are suitable for groups of twelve or more. Place chairs so that each participant faces the front of the room.

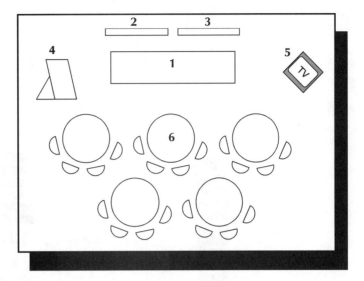

Legend

1. Facilitator's table
2. Whiteboard
3. Projection screen
4. Flipchart stand
5. Video player/monitor
6. Participant tables and seating

Audiovisual equipment

The facilitator's table, easels, and videocassette player should be positioned for clear viewing by all participants. The sound system should be adjusted so that everyone can hear films and videos (if used) or words spoken into a microphone.

Power source

Find out where the climate control, light switches, electrical outlets, and sound system controls are. Also, obtain the name of the technician to call if you need assistance.

Supplies and refreshments

Place one table to the side for materials, supplies, and items such as a three-hole punch, stapler, and staple puller. If refreshments will be served, set those up on a second side table.

Facilities

Locate the phones, restrooms, vending machines, and cafeteria so that you can direct participants to them. Get names of nearby lunch spots if lunch is not provided.

Name Tent

Teambuilding Workshop

Participant Name

Teambuilding Workshop

Participant Name

Announcing the Workshop

Announce the workshop at least four weeks prior to the scheduled date. You can publicize the program via memos, letters, E-mail, voice mail, personal phone calls, announcements at meetings, employee newspaper, or management bulletin. Include the following information:

- Workshop title.
- Date and hours of the workshop.
- Location.
- Description.
- Objectives.
- Key topics.
- Prerequisites (if any).
- Facilitator's name and brief statement of credentials.
- Cost.
- How to apply.
- Application deadline.

Sample Announcements

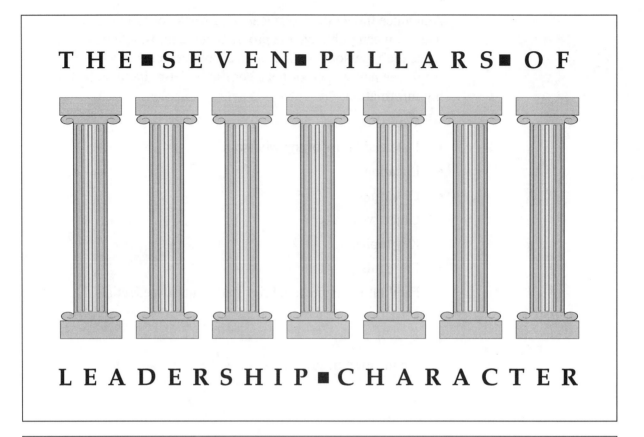

Workshop Follow-Up

There is no doubt that post-workshop follow-up activities can enhance the value of the workshop experience. Orchestrating these activities is another issue. Participants can work on their issues past the session's ending. It is recommended that they make a commitment to one another to continue working on the issues that surface in the training. Here are some thoughts about follow-up.

- Have participants work on issues with workshop partners over a ninety-day period for support.

- Have participants work together as a team when possible for continued development.

- Encourage the exchange of information about particpant needs.

Now, before we move on to the next chapter, let's make sure that you are ready for the sessions.

Prepare for a Successful Event!

Once you have completed the tasks described in this chapter and the appropriate workshop chapter, you will be ready to conduct each session. Here are just a few suggestions that might be helpful.

- Review your notes and other information that you gathered during your planning session to ensure that the sessions will meet the needs of your participants.

- Use your checklists to ensure that all the pre-work is accomplished.

- Be sure that you are familiar with the facility in which you will conduct the training.

The Bottom-Line . . .

- Be prepared.

- Maintain a positive frame of reference.

- Stay aware of the information that you share.

- Stay on time.

- Maintain a high energy level.

- Be flexible and adjust to the team's rhythm.

Workshop Certificate

Certificate of Achievement

This certifies that

_____

(name)

successfully completed the

Teambuilding Workshop

on

_____

(date)

Congratulations!

(Facilitator)

(Training Manager)

Chapter Four:

One-Hour Teambuilding Workshop

This chapter contains the training plan for your one-hour team-building exercise—ready to go "as is" or to be tailored to meet your needs. It is intended to be used in conjunction with one or both of the training designs that follow. The chapter is divided into three parts:

* Materials Needed

* Tailoring Tips

* Training Plan

"THE TEAM BUILDING INSTRUMENT"

This workshop is designed to give the trainer a picture of areas that need addressing in the team. With this picture the trainer can then individualize the training effort, giving particular attention to the specific area, or areas, that need improvement.

The participants will, by taking the instrument, give the trainer an idea as to exactly which area the team should spend time on in the half-day or one-day workshop .

Materials Needed

These are the materials recommended for the *One-Hour Team-building Workshop*. Page references indicate where masters for the materials are found elsewhere in this book. Unless otherwise noted:

•   Make one copy per participant, plus a few spares.

Trainer's Notes

☐ Team Building Instrument (TBI) (pp. 215-216)

Tools and Assessments

☐ Team Building Instrument (TBI) (pp. 218-219)

☐ TBI Scoring Grid (p. 220)

Overhead Transparencies

☐ None

Suggested flipcharts   The following flipcharts are used in the one-hour workshop.

☐ Teambuilding Model

☐ Team Insights and Issues

Teambuilding Model

• Team Purpose
• Stages of Team Development
• Team Member Roles
• Team Communication
• Team Processes
• Team Leadership

Team Insights and Issues

(summarize responses from group discussion)

Tailoring Tips

To tailor the workshop to your particular group, do the following:

- For ease in distributing and referring to materials in class, create a numbered handout packet that has been bound or stapled.

- Design a custom cover with the name of the sponsoring organization, date, and place of the workshop, printed on heavy paper (cover stock).

- Distribute the packet when you begin the workshop and refer participants to appropriate pages throughout the day.

Things to do   Prior to conducting the workshop, do the following:

 Read Chapter 4: "One-Hour Teambuilding Workshop."

 Review the Team Building Instrument
Completely familiarize yourself with the scoring process for the instrument.

 Prepare Materials.
Photocopy the following:

- The workshop agenda and script. Write your planned start/stop times and anecdotal material on the photocopy.

- Copies of the instrument for participants.

 Inquire About Special Needs.
Meet with the director of training and several of the individuals enrolled in the course to learn about any special needs, internal issues, and the experience level of participants.

 Develop Relevant Examples.
Develop examples that are relevant to the industry or enterprise.

 Encourage Management Participation.
Invite a middle or top manager to kick off the workshop and emphasize the important role supervisors play.

Training Plan

Purpose

To give the trainer a picture of areas that need addressing in the team. The trainer can then individualize the training effort, giving particular attention to the specific area, or areas, that need improvement.

Overview

The *Team Building Instrument* (TBI) is designed to examine individual perceptions of team strengths and weaknesses in the following six areas related to team development:

- Team Purpose

- Stages of Team Development

- Team Member Roles

- Team Communication

- Team Processes

- Team Leadership

The results identify specific areas where teambuilding efforts can be focused.

Workshop Agenda

The Team Building Instrument (TBI)	Minutes 60	Start / Stop 8:00 / 9:00	Actual Start / Stop
Introduction	10	8:00 / 8:10	_____ / _____
Objectives	10	8:10 / 8:20	_____ / _____
Survey Completion 1. Administer 2. Scoring	20	8:20 / 8:40	_____ / _____
Group Discussion	10	8:40 / 8:50	_____ / _____
Key Points/Summary	10	8:50 / 9:00	_____ / _____

The Team Building Instrument (8:00 to 9:00)

FACILITATOR COMMENTARY

00:10   **Introduction**

INTRODUCE the instrument, explaining the purpose.

GROUP DISCUSSION

00:10   **Objectives**

DISPLAY the flipchart, *Teambuilding Model* (p. 76), showing the six areas of team development this model addresses. Explain that the six areas are the basic building blocks of teams and will be assessed in an instrument. The outcomes will direct the team's efforts in improvement.

OVERVIEW the six basic areas:

- Team Purpose
- Stages of Team Development
- Team Member Roles
- Team Communication
- Team Processes
- Team Leadership

EMPHASIZE the following:

The instrument can help the team locate the areas that need addressing, in order to grow in a healthy and constructive way.

ASK if there are any questions regarding the instrument. If there are, address them in a timely fashion. If there are no questions start the instrument.

Notes

- _____
- _____
- _____
- _____
- _____
- _____

GROUP ACTIVITY

00:20   **Survey Completion**

 DISTRIBUTE copies of the *Team Building Instrument* (TBI) (pp. 218-219) and the *TBI Scoring Grid* (p. 220). Reiterate that this will give a view of the areas the team should address to be more effective.

 EXPLAIN the marking of the instrument, noting that they check either Agree or Disagree for each question. At the end of each section they will total their responses.

 EXPLAIN the operation of the *TBI Scoring Grid*. Transfer all scores from the end of each section to the grid. This grid can now be used to interpret the areas that require addressing. Note that high Disagree ratings invite the team to look at areas for improvement.

Option   Combine all team members' scores onto one grid. An example would be of a master grid with everyone's score in it. The master grid would look like the following:

	Agree	Disagree	Total*
Team Purpose	18	22	40
Stages of Development	19	21	40
Team Member Roles	30	10	40
Team Communication	32	8	40
Team Processes	7	33	40
Team Leadership	28	12	40

The number for each section is the total number of Agrees or Disagrees for the entire team. Eight team members times five responses would give a total for each section of forty. The higher the disagree score the more significant the area.

 EXPLAIN that this is one way to look at the team. The master grid enables the team to see itself as a whole. This knowledge might, or might not, correlate with the individual scoring. As the individual sees things in a personal way, when you look at the whole, you might see that everyone else in the team sees it differently.

In the example above we can see one area that stands out—Team Processes. As an individual, one person may not have had that as the high area. Yet as a team it indicates an area that needs to be addressed.

GROUP DISCUSSION

00:10   **Team Insights or Issues**

 DISCUSS the results from the instrument. Has the team learned anything from the results?

 RECORD responses on the *Team Insights or Issues* flipchart (p. 76).

 ASK the following questions to generate discussion, or for thought starters:

- What does this say about the team?

- What areas should the team focus on?

- Is there one area that stands out from all the rest?

- Can you see any differences between individual scores?

- What area(s) should the team work on?

FACILITATOR COMMENTARY

00:10   **Key Points/Summary**

 SUMMARIZE these key points:

- The instrument gives us a view of the areas that should be addressed through further teambuilding activities.

- The team can look in each section to detail the areas that stand out.

- The team now has insight as to the areas that it can improve upon.

 The following flowchart is for the facilitator's use and shows how to incorporate the TBI with planning a workshop. You may use any combination of modules to fit either a one-hour, half-day, or one-day program. The modules are indepenent of one another and can be used alone or in combination with each other. The combination of modules can be used in any manner appropriate to the team's needs.

TEAMBUILDING
WORKSHOP FLOWCHART

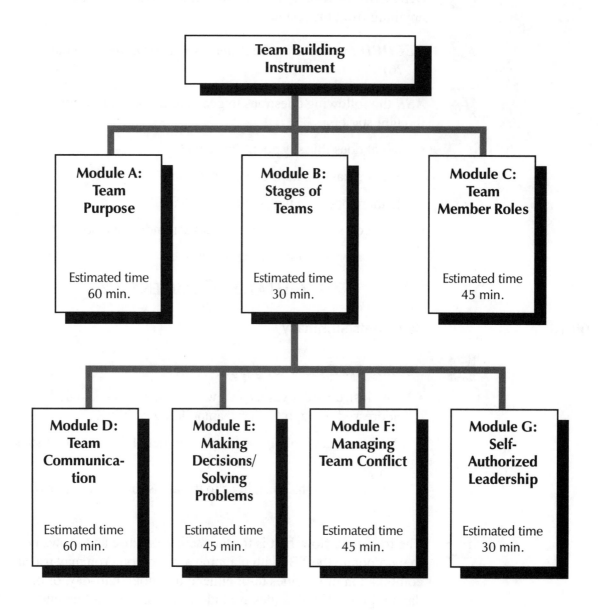

**Team Building
Instrument**

**Module A:
Team
Purpose**

Estimated time
60 min.

**Module B:
Stages of
Teams**

Estimated time
30 min.

**Module C:
Team
Member Roles**

Estimated time
45 min.

**Module D:
Team
Communica-
tion**

Estimated time
60 min.

**Module E:
Making
Decisions/
Solving
Problems**

Estimated time
45 min.

**Module F:
Managing
Team Conflict**

Estimated time
45 min.

**Module G:
Self-
Authorized
Leadership**

Estimated time
30 min.

Chapter Five:

Half-Day Teambuilding Workshop

This chapter contains the training plan for a half-day teambuilding workshop—ready to go "as is" or to be tailored to meet your needs. The chapter is divided into three parts:

- Workshop Agenda

- Materials Needed

- Training Plan

"STAGES OF TEAM DEVELOPMENT"

This program explores the different stages of team develop ment, the roles members operate in, and how these along with their communication processes, affect team perfo r-mance.

When participants have completed this workshop they will be able to:

- Identify stages of team developmen t.

- Identify the current stage of the team .

- Identify and use the proper roles in their team structure .

- Explain the dynamics of interchangeable roles .

- Identify task and process language as indicators of team communication style .

- Identify barriers to the team's communication process.

- Practice strategies for giving and receiving feedback in order to improve team communication .

- Determine the source of conflict that arises in teams .

Workshop Agenda

1. Stages of Team Development	Minutes 40	Start / Stop 8:00 / 8:40	Actual Start / Stop
Introduction	5	8:00 / 8:05	_____ / _____
Stages of Teams	5	8:05 / 8:10	_____ / _____
Characteristics of Stages • Forming • Storming • Norming • Performing	5	8:10 / 8:15	_____ / _____
Group Activity: Team Rating Form	10	8:15 / 8:25	_____ / _____
Group Discussion	10	8:25 / 8:35	_____ / _____
Key Points/Summary	5	8:35 / 8:40	_____ / _____

2. Team Member Roles	Minutes 50	Start / Stop 8:40 / 9:30	Actual Start / Stop
Introduction	5	8:40 / 8:45	_____ / _____
Task/Process Model • Task Roles • Process Roles	10	8:45 / 8:55	_____ / _____
Group Activity: Role Identification	15	8:55 / 9:10	_____ / _____
Group Discussion	15	9:10 / 9:25	_____ / _____
Key Points/Summary	5	9:25 / 9:30	_____ / _____
Break	15	9:30 / 9:45	_____ / _____

3. Team Communications	Minutes 60	Start / Stop 9:45 / 10:45	Actual Start / Stop
Introduction	5	9:45 / 9:50	_____ / _____
Communication Process • Task Communication • Process Communication • Barriers to Communication	20	9:50 / 10:10	_____ / _____
Group Activity • Giving Feedback • Receiving Feedback	15	10:10 / 10:25	_____ / _____
Group Discussion	15	10:25 / 10:40	_____ / _____
Key Points/Summary	5	10:40 / 10:45	_____ / _____

4. Managing Team Conflicts	Minutes 50	Start / Stop 10:45 / 11:35	Actual Start / Stop
Introduction	5	10:45 / 10:50	_____ / _____
Causes of Conflict	5	10:50 / 10:55	_____ / _____
Conflict Management Strategies • Competition • Collaboration • Avoidance • Accommodation • Compromise	15	10:55 / 11:10	_____ / _____
Group Activity: Conflict Resolution	10	11:10 / 11:20	_____ / _____
Group Discussion	10	11:20 / 11:30	_____ / _____
Key Points/Summary	5	11:30 / 11:35	_____ / _____

Materials Needed

The following materials are recommended for the *Half-Day Teambuilding Workshop*. Page references indicate where masters for the materials are found elsewhere in this book. Unless otherwise noted:

- For overhead transparencies, you will need one transparency each.

- For other items, you will need one per participant, plus a few spares.

Overhead Transparencies

- ☐ Stages of Team Development (p. 239)
- ☐ Forming Stage (p. 240)
- ☐ Storming Stage (p. 241)
- ☐ Norming Stage (p. 242)
- ☐ Performing Stage (p. 243)
- ☐ Team Member Roles (p. 244)
- ☐ Task Roles (p. 245)
- ☐ Process Roles (p. 246)
- ☐ Dysfunctional Team Member Behavior (p. 247)
- ☐ Responses to Dysfunctional Behaviors (p. 248)
- ☐ Communication Process (p. 249)
- ☐ Process Communication (p. 252)
- ☐ Task Communication (p. 250)
- ☐ Communication Barriers (p. 254)
- ☐ Overcoming Communication Barriers (p. 255)
- ☐ Benefits of Giving Feedback (p. 256)
- ☐ Causes of Team Conflict (p. 264)
- ☐ Competition (p. 266)
- ☐ Collaboration (p. 267)
- ☐ Avoidance (p. 268)
- ☐ Accommodation (p. 269)
- ☐ Compromise (p. 270)
- ☐ Steps to Managing Team Conflict (p. 271)

Handouts

- ☐ Stages of Team Development (p. 152)
- ☐ Stage 1: Forming (p. 153)
- ☐ Stage 2: Storming (p. 154)
- ☐ Stage 3: Norming (p. 155)
- ☐ Stage 4: Performing (p. 156)
- ☐ Group Development Models (p. 157)
- ☐ Team Member Roles (p. 158)
- ☐ Task Roles (p. 159)
- ☐ Process Roles (p. 160)
- ☐ Task and Process Involvement Model (p. 161)
- ☐ Giving Feedback (p. 167)
- ☐ Giving Feedback to Others (p. 168)
- ☐ Receiving Feedback from Others (optional) (p. 169)

Tools and Assessments

- ☐ Team Development Rating Form (pp. 230-231)

Tailoring Tips

To tailor the workshop to your particular group, do the following:

- For ease in distributing and referring to materials in class, create a numbered handout packet. Bind or staple the packet.

- Design a custom cover with the name of the sponsoring organization, date, and place of the workshop, and print it on heavy paper (cover stock).

- Distribute the packet when you begin the workshop and refer participants to appropriate pages throughout the day.

Things to do   Prior to conducting the workshop, do the following:

 Review Chapter 5: The Half-Day Teambuilding Worksho p

Refer to the overheads and handouts as you review the plans. Read the preparation section of each module and follow the instructions.

 Prepare Materials

Photocopy the following:

- The workshop agenda and script. Write your planned start/stop times and anecdotal material on the photocopy.

- Overheads.

- Participant handouts.

Prepare flipcharts using the handouts listed below and the examples on pages 88 and 89.

It is helpful to leave several blank pages between the prepared pages for use during the workshop and to avoid displaying the next item before the appropriate time.

- *Group Development Models* (p. 157).

- *Task and Process Involvement Model* (p. 161).

 Inquire About Special Need s

Meet with the director of training and several of the individuals enrolled in the course to learn about any special needs, internal issues, and the experience level of participants.

 Develop Relevant Example s

Develop examples that are relevant to the industry or enterprise.

 Encourage Management Participatio n

Invite a middle or top manager to kick off the workshop and emphasize the important role supervisors play.

Suggested Flipcharts

1.

Group Development Models

Theories	Stage 1	Stage 2	Stage 3	Stage 4
Bennis Sheppard	Dependence	Counter-Dependence	Resolution	Inter-Dependence
Gibb	Acceptance	Data Flow	Goals and Norms	Control
Schutz	Inclusion	Control	Openness	Deinclusion
Tuckman	Forming	Storming	Norming	Performing
Kormanski Mozenter	Awareness	Conflict	Cooperation	Productivity
Varney	Formation	Building	Working	Maturity

2.

Team Stages

(Record team observations here.)

3.

Stages of Team Development

Stages:

- Forming
- Norming
- Storming
- Performing

4.

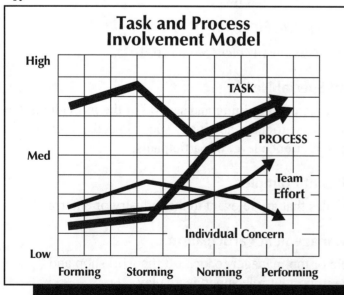

Task and Process Involvement Model

5.

Examples of Roles

Task:

- Information giver
- Opinion giver
- Standard setter

Process:

- Encourager
- Gatekeeper
- Listener

6.

What Are Your Roles?

Roles:

(Record team
observations here.)

7.

Task and Process Statements

Task:

- What?
- Why?
- I think that . . .

Process:

- How?
- I feel . . .

8.

Giving Feedback

(Record responses from
group discussion here.)

9.

Managing Conflict

- Competition
- Collaboration
- Avoidance
- Accommodation
- Compromise

Training Plan

Stages of Team Development

Purpose   This module explains the different stages of growth/change that a team goes through, and how these stages affect the team output and internal cohesion.

Prework   Read *Stages of Team Development* (pp. 22-27). Prepare the *Group Development Models* flipchart.

Workshop Agenda

1. Stages of Team Development	Minutes 40	Start / Stop 8:00 / 8:40	Actual Start / Stop
Introduction	5	8:00 / 8:05	_____ / _____
Stages of Teams	5	8:05 / 8:10	_____ / _____
Characteristics of Stages • Forming • Storming • Norming • Performing	5	8:10 / 8:15	_____ / _____
Group Activity: Team Rating Form	10	8:15 / 8:25	_____ / _____
Group Discussion	10	8:25 / 8:35	_____ / _____
Key Points/Summary	5	8:35 / 8:40	_____ / _____

1. Stages of Team Development (8:00 to 8:40)

FACILITATOR COMMENTARY

00:05   **Introduction**

INTRODUCE the module and explain the purpose.

REVIEW the *Stages of Team Development* results from the *Team Building Instrument* (TBI) to set the tone for what the team may need help with. Ask members to reflect on which stage they are in, based upon the results of the survey.

00:05   **Stages of Teams**

DISTRIBUTE the handout, *Stages of Team Development* (p. 152).

DESCRIBE the stages of team development (p. 22) and *REFER* to the overhead, *Stages of Team Development* (p. 239).

Note: These stages are based upon Tuckman's model for team development.

00:05   **Characteristics of Stages**

DISTRIBUTE the handouts, *Stage 1: Forming, Stage 2: Storming, Stage 3: Norming,* and *Stage 4: Performing* (pp. 153-156).

DETAIL each stage using pages 23-27 and the overheads on pages 240-243.

- Forming
- Storming
- Norming
- Performing

DISCUSS examples of each stage.

WRITE teams observations of stages on the flipchart, *Team Stages*.

ASK the following questions to generate discussion, or for thought starters.

- What stage does the team think they are in now?
- Why does the team think they are in this stage?
- What teams do you see that are stuck in certain stages?

DISCUSS any differences in the group, searching for agreement on the resolution of any differences that exist.

 ADJUST the team observations on the flipchart to reflect group agreement.

 POST the *Team Stages* flipchart.

GROUP ACTIVITY

00:10   **Team Development Rating**

 REFER to the Trainers Notes for *Team Development Rating Form* (p. 230), and *DISTRIBUTE* the *Team Development Rating Form* (p. 231).

GROUP DISCUSSION

00:10   **Group Discussion of Scores**

 DISCUSS the results of this activity and share with the entire team.

 ASK the following questions to generate discussion, or for thought starters.

- Where does the team go from here?
- What do these scores mean?
- Is there any disagreement in the team now?
- How is work done in the team?
- What are your stages?

 WRITE responses on the flipchart, *Stages of Team Development* under the heading "Stages."

FACILITATOR COMMENTARY

00:05   **Key Points/Summary**

SUMMARIZE these key points.

- All teams go through these stages.
- The stages are experienced in sequential order.
- New members will cause the team to start over.

Team Member Roles

Purpose

In teams we see that team dynamics consist of task and process roles. Each member will, at certain times, play these roles. We will learn what will happen to a team if these roles are played but not at the right time, as well as when the roles are correctly played.

Objectives

After completion of this module, the participants will be able to:

- Identify task and process roles played by team members.

- Understand their influence on team performance.

Workshop Agenda

2. Team Member Roles	Minutes 50	Start / Stop 8:40 / 9:30	Actual Start / Stop
Introduction	5	8:40 / 8:45	_____ / _____
Task/Process Model • Task Roles • Process Roles	10	8:45 / 8:55	_____ / _____
Group Activity: Role Identification	15	8:55 / 9:10	_____ / _____
Group Discussion	15	9:10 / 9:25	_____ / _____
Key Points/Summary	5	9:25 / 9:30	_____ / _____
Break	15	9:30 / 9:45	_____ / _____

2. Team Member Roles (8:40 to 9:30)

FACILITATOR COMMENTARY

00:05   **Introduction**

INTRODUCE the module and explain the purpose.

REVIEW the *Team Member Roles* results from the *Team Building Instrument*. Ask members to reflect on the roles they play in their team as they review the survey results.

DISTRIBUTE the handouts *Team Member Roles* (p. 158), *Task Roles* (p. 159) and *Process Roles* (p. 160).

00:10   **Task/Process Model**

DESCRIBE and explain the task/process model using the *Team Member Roles* overhead (p. 244). Distinguish between task and process.

DESCRIBE the different task roles (p. 30) using the *Task Roles* overhead (p. 245).

DESCRIBE the different process roles (p. 31) using the *Process Roles* overhead (p. 246).

SHOW the flipchart, *Examples of Roles*.

ASK for examples of different teams in the task and process roles, probing for several examples of each.

WRITE the team observations of the different roles members play on the flipchart.

ASK the following questions to generate discussion, or for thought starters.

- How does this correlate to what we found out in the stages of team development?

- What is useful about being task focused?

- What is useful about being process focused?

- What are some disadvantages from being in one mode too frequently?

POST the responses to the above questions on a flipchart.

GROUP ACTIVITY

00:15   **Role Identification**

 ASK group members to identify three or four roles they have played recently or seen played by other team members.

EXPLAIN that each team member plays these roles at different times during a meeting. The purpose of this activity is to show how these roles shift.

SHOW the overhead, *Dysfunctional Team Member Behaviors* (p. 247).

DESCRIBE dysfunctional behavior (p. 33) being careful not to personalize the issue. Ask how the team will deal with dysfunctional behavior when it does arise.

SHOW the overhead, *Responses to Dysfunctional Behavior* (p. 248).

GROUP DISCUSSION

00:15   **Role Identification Summary**

ASK the following process learning questions:

- How will the team deal with the dysfunctional roles?

- How will the team deal with someone being too oriented to one style or the other?

- How will the team apply their knowledge so they may function better?

SHOW the flipchart, *What Are Your Roles?*

WRITE responses on the flipchart, under the heading "Roles."

FACILITATOR COMMENTARY

00:05

Key Points/Summary

SUMMARIZE these key points.

- All teams have people in different roles at different times.
- Sometimes the roles are played dysfunctionally.
- Team members must have ways to deal with dysfunctional behaviors, or risk destroying the team.
- Team output is maximized by playing the correct roles at the correct times.
- New members will cause the team to start over.

00:15

Break

Notes

- _____

- _____

- _____

- _____

- _____

- _____

- _____

- _____

- _____

- _____

- _____

- _____

- _____

- _____

- _____

- _____

- _____

Team Communication

Purpose   Examine the critical importance of communication to effective teamwork, identifying strategies for improving the communication process.

Objectives   After completion of this module, the participants will be able to:

- Identify task and process communication methods used by team members.

- Appreciate the value of both methods of communication.

Workshop Agenda

3. Team Communications	Minutes 60	Start / Stop 9:45 / 10:45	Actual Start / Stop
Introduction	5	9:45 / 9:50	_____ / _____
Communication Process • Task Communication • Process Communication • Barriers to Communication	20	9:50 / 10:10	_____ / _____
Group Activity • Giving Feedback • Receiving Feedback	15	10:10 / 10:25	_____ / _____
Group Discussion	15	10:25 / 10:40	_____ / _____
Key Points/Summary	5	10:40 / 10:45	_____ / _____

3. Team Communication (9:45 to 10:45)

FACILITATOR COMMENTARY

00:05   **Introduction**

INTRODUCE the module and explain the purpose. Emphasize that the quality of a team's work depends largely upon the quality of their information process.

REVIEW the *Team Communication* results from the *Team Building Instrument* to set the tone for what the team may need help with, based upon the survey results.

00:20   **Communication Process**

SHOW the overhead, *Communication Process* (p. 249).

DESCRIBE the communication process:

- Communication is an exchange of information, which is transmitted, received, and acted upon.

- Sender must encode or translate thoughts into symbols.

- Message is sent verbally, electronically, or through writing.

- Receiver must decode or translate the message.

- When translation is accurate, effective communication occurs.

- Since people attach different meanings or translations, problems can occur.

Refer to Chapter 2 (pp. 35-36) for explanations of key points.

ASK members to reflect on how effectively they are communicating and what the stage of the team's development is.

EXPLAIN that a team's language often reflects its state of development. Communication can be characterized as task or process. A mismatch of process and task language can create miscommunication.

SHOW the overhead, *Task Communication* (p. 250) and *DESCRIBE* *Task Communication* (p. 37).

The background information in Chapter 2, *Stages of Team Development* and *Team Member Roles* (pp. 29-32), provides information on task and process which links to this section. Actively build upon these two.

SHOW the overhead, *Process Communication* (p. 252) and *DESCRIBE* process communication (p. 38).

 ASK the group for examples of task and process statements, writing them on the flipchart, *Task and Process Statements*, and underlining the key words. Have some of your own examples in mind, to stimulate the group if necessary. Guide the class in reviewing the statements and evaluating them according to the communication characteristics.

 SHOW the overhead, *Communication Barriers* (p. 254) and *DESCRIBE* barriers to effective team communication (p. 39).

 SHOW the overhead, *Overcoming Communication Barriers* (p. 255) and *DESCRIBE* strategies for overcoming communication barriers (p. 41).

 DISCUSS how task and process statements can create barriers, depending on the receiver and how to overcome them by different types of responses. Explore how understanding the two response types can enhance the team communication process.

 WRITE the responses on a flipchart.

GROUP ACTIVITY

00:15   **Giving Feedback**

 DESCRIBE giving and receiving feedback:

- Almost all aspects of team communication involve feedback.

- Smart members solicit feedback about their own behavior.

- Giving and receiving feedback effectively is a skill.

 EXPLAIN the purpose of the activity: to explore guidelines for effective feedback to help the team strengthen their communication process.

 DISPLAY the overhead, *Benefits of Giving Feedback* (p. 256) and *DISTRIBUTE* a copy of *Giving Feedback* (p. 167) to each team member.

 ASK them to select the features they believe are most characteristic of their team.

GROUP DISCUSSION

00:15   **Giving Feedback**

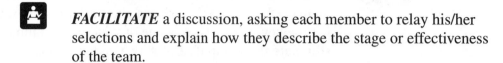 *FACILITATE* a discussion, asking each member to relay his/her selections and explain how they describe the stage or effectiveness of the team.

WRITE the responses on the flipchart, *Giving Feedback.*

Prepare a simple matrix and note their key ideas by each feature.

DISTRIBUTE the handouts, *Giving Feedback to Others* (p. 168) and *Receiving Feedback from Others* (p. 169) to each team member.

REVIEW the posted information with the members, and determine which features they believe would most effectively guide their team at their current stage of development.

DISCUSS guidelines and benefits for giving feedback in a team (p. 44).

If time allows, discuss the notion of reasonable feedback—that which deals with behavior that can be changed by recipient, as opposed to behavior that is out of recipient's control.

DESCRIBE the guidelines for receiving feedback (p. 45).

Continue the activity and discussion for receiving feedback. Conduct the activity and discussion the same as for giving feedback.

FACILITATOR COMMENTARY

00:05   **Key Points/Summary**

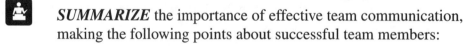 *SUMMARIZE* the importance of effective team communication, making the following points about successful team members:

- They are aware of their language and its impact on others.

- They use validated techniques for giving and receiving feedback as a tool:

  - for developing open channels of communication.

  - for enhancing the flexibility and performance of the team.

Managing Team Conflict

Purpose   Explore the causes of team conflict and five strategies for managing conflict.

Objectives   After completion of this module, the participants will be able to:

- Understand the causes of team conflict.

- Learn effective strategies for managing conflict.

Workshop Agenda

4. Managing Team Conflict	Minutes 50	Start / Stop 10:45 / 11:35	Actual Start / Stop
Introduction	5	10:45 / 10:50	_____ / _____
Causes of Conflict	5	10:50 / 10:55	_____ / _____
Conflict Management Strategies • Competition • Collaboration • Avoidance • Accommodation • Compromise	15	10:55 / 11:10	_____ / _____
Group Activity: Conflict Resolution	10	11:10 / 11:20	_____ / _____
Group Discussion	10	11:20 / 11:30	_____ / _____
Key Points/Summary	5	11:30 / 11:35	_____ / _____

4. Managing Team Conflict (10:45 to 11:35)

FACILITATOR COMMENTARY

00:05   **Introduction**

INTRODUCE the module and explain the purpose. Emphasize that the quality of a team's work depends largely upon the quality of their information process.

EMPHASIZE that the ability to resolve team conflict is the most important skill team members can develop.

REVIEW the results from the *Team Building Instrument* to set the tone for what the team may need help with, based upon the survey. Ask members to reflect on how effectively they are managing conflict, based upon the results of the survey.

00:05   **Causes of Conflict**

SHOW the overhead, *Causes of Team Conflict* (p. 264).

ASK participants to name possible sources of team conflict, and lead into describing these five causes:

- Personality differences.

- Values differences.

- Differences in perspective.

- Differences in goals.

- Cultural differences.

DISCUSS team members' perspectives of the causes, and how their conflict is a result of these causes.

LINK the stage of the team's development and how this may be reflected in their team conflict *temperature*. (Storming usually involves considerable conflict).

FACILITATOR COMMENTARY

00:15   **Conflict Management Strategies**

EXPLAIN that conflict is natural, but resolving it is a skill—as a transition into the five strategies for managing conflict (p. 53).

SHOW the overheads, *Competition* (p. 266), *Collaboration* (p. 267), *Avoidance* (p. 268), *Accommodation* (p. 269), and *Compromise* (p. 270).

 DETAIL each strategy. *USE* the flipchart, *Managing Conflict,* and pages 52-54.

- Competition.
- Collaboration.
- Avoidance.
- Accommodation.
- Compromise.

ASK the group to name situations of conflict present in the team.

WRITE the responses on the flipchart.

ASK the group to review the situations and determine which strategy is most appropriate in each situation.

REVIEW the overhead that summarizes each strategy.

DESCRIBE the steps to manage team conflict, as a possible model for the team, using (p. 52). Transition to the activity as a way for the team to practice the steps.

GROUP ACTIVITY

00:10   **Conflict Resolution**

EXPLAIN the purpose of the activity: to practice managing conflict, and to help the team strengthen their skills.

SHOW the overhead, *Steps to Managing Team Conflict* (p. 271) for reference.

Remind them to use the guidelines for useful feedback (p. 42).

Select an actual team conflict situation from the list generated earlier. Guide the group through the steps.

WRITE the outcomes of each step on the flipchart.

Identify which conflict management strategy would be most appropriate in this situation.

GROUP DISCUSSION

00:10   **Conflict Resolution**

DISCUSS and review the posted information with the team members.

- How did it go? What worked? What could be improved in their application of the model?

- Did their selected conflict strategy apply to the situation? How does the strategy reflect their team's current stage of development?

- How will they implement the solution?

- How can they remember to apply this management system with future conflicts?

POST the *Managing Conflict* flipchart.

FACILITATOR COMMENTARY

00:05   **Key Points/Summary**

MAKE these key points to summarize the benefits of successfully using team conflicts.

- Conflict is useful when viewed as an opportunity for discussing and managing problems, which are inevitable in human relationships.

- The quality of decision making can be improved by allowing different points of view to be examined.

- Conflict is healthy when effectively managed. It is an antidote for "group think." It does not allow the team to passively accept decisions that may be based on incomplete or inappropriate information. It challenges the status quo and facilitates the consideration of new ideas.

Chapter Six:

One-Day Teambuilding Workshop

This chapter contains the training plan for a one-day teambuilding workshop—ready to go "as is" or to be tailored to meet your needs. The chapter is divided into three parts:

- Workshop Agenda

- Materials Needed

- Training Plan

"TEAM PURPOSE"

This program is composed of seven training modules :
- Team Purpose
- Stages of Team Development
- Team Member Roles
- Team Communication
- Decision Making and Problem Solving
- Managing Team Conflicts
- Self-Authorized Team Leadership

After completing the workshop, participants will be able to :

- Describe the characteristics of a team mission statement and use the criteria to develop effective team goals .

- Identify stages of team development and use the proper roles in their team structure.

- Explain the dynamics of interchangeable roles and identify task and process language as indicators of team communication style.

- Identify barriers to the team's communication process and practice strategies for giving and receiving feedback in order to improve team communication.

- Explain the difference between decision making and problem solving and identify the proper process to use in the team.

- Determine the source of conflict that arises in teams and practice strategies for dealing with team conflict.

- Emulate the characteristics of self-leadership .

Workshop Agenda

1. Team Purpose	Minutes 45	Start / Stop 8:00 / 8:45	Actual Start / Stop
Introduction	5	8:00 / 8:05	_____ / _____
Mission Statements • Criteria of Statements • Mission Formulation	15	8:05 / 8:20	_____ / _____
Goals • Team Goals • Goal Characteristics	10	8:20 / 8:30	_____ / _____
Group Discussion	10	8:30 / 8:40	_____ / _____
Key Points/Summary	5	8:40 / 8:45	_____ / _____

2. Stages of Team Development	Minutes 40	Start / Stop 8:45 / 9:25	Actual Start / Stop
Introduction	5	8:45 / 8:50	_____ / _____
Stages of Teams	5	8:50 / 8:55	_____ / _____
Characteristics of Stages: • Forming • Storming • Norming • Performing	5	8:55 / 9:00	_____ / _____
Group Activity: Team Rating Form	10	9:00 / 9:10	_____ / _____
Group Discussion	10	9:10 / 9:20	_____ / _____
Key Points/Summary	5	9:20 / 9:25	_____ / _____
Break	10	9:25 / 9:35	_____ / _____

3. Team Member Roles	Minutes 50	Start / Stop 9:35 / 10:25	Actual Start / Stop
Introduction	5	9:35 / 9:40	_____ / _____
Task/Process Model • Task Roles • Process Roles	10	9:40 / 9:50	_____ / _____
Group Activity: Role Identification	15	9:50 / 10:05	_____ / _____
Group Discussion	15	10:05 / 10:20	_____ / _____
Key Points/Summary	5	10:20 / 10:25	_____ / _____

4. Team Communication	Minutes 60	Start / Stop 10:25 / 11:25	Actual Start / Stop
Introduction	5	10:25 / 10:30	_____ / _____
Communication Process • Task Communication • Process Communication • Barriers to Communication	20	10:30 / 10:50	
Group Activity • Giving Feedback • Receiving Feedback	15	10:50 / 11:05	_____ / _____
Group Discussion	15	11:05 / 11:20	_____ / _____
Key Points/Summary	5	11:20 / 11:25	_____ / _____
Lunch	60	11:25 / 12:55	_____ / _____

5. Decision Making/Problem Solving	Minutes 60	Start / Stop 12:25 / 1:25	Actual Start / Stop
Introduction	5	12:25 / 12:30	_____ / _____
Decision Making Model	5	12:30 / 12:35	_____ / _____
Characteristics of Decisions: • Different Types of Decisions • Decision Model • Decision Making Procedures • Problem Solving Steps	15	12:35 / 12:50	_____ / _____
Group Activity: • Problem Identification	15	12:50 / 1:05	_____ / _____
Group Discussion	15	1:05 / 1:20	_____ / _____
Key Points/Summary	5	1:20 / 1:25	_____ / _____

6. Managing Team Conflict	Minutes 1 hr 5	Start / Stop 1:25 / 2:45	Actual Start / Stop
Introduction	5	1:25 / 1:30	_____ / _____
Causes of Conflict	5	1:30 / 1:35	_____ / _____
Conflict Management Strategies: • Competition • Collaboration • Avoidance • Accommodation • Compromise	20	1:35 / 1:55	_____ / _____
Group Activity: Conflict Resolution	15	1:55 / 2:10	_____ / _____
Group Discussion	15	2:10 / 2:25	_____ / _____
Key Points/Summary	5	2:25 / 2:30	_____ / _____
Break	15	2:30 / 2:45	_____ / _____

7. Self-Authorized Team Leadership	Minutes 50	Start / Stop 2:45/ 3:45	Actual Start / Stop
Introduction	5	2:45 / 2:50	_____ / _____
Self-Authorized Team Leadership	5	2:50 / 2:55	_____ / _____
Strategies: • Behavioral • Cognitive • Increasing Leadership Effectiveness • Seven Pillars of Leadership	15	2:55 / 3:10	_____ / _____
Group Activity: • Leadership Role Checklist	15	3:10 / 3:25	_____ / _____
Group Discussion	15	3:25 / 3:40	_____ / _____
Key Points/Summary	5	3:40 / 3:45	_____ / _____

Materials Needed

These materials are recommended for the One-Day Teambuilding Workshop. Page references indicate where masters for the materials are found in this book. Unless otherwise noted:

- For overhead transparencies, you will need one transparency each.
- For other items, you will need one per participant, plus a few spares.

Overhead Transparencies

- ☐ Task Communication (p. 250)
- ☐ Process Communication (p. 252)
- ☐ Causes of Team Conflict (p. 264)
- ☐ Competition (p. 266)
- ☐ Collaboration (p. 267)
- ☐ Avoidance (p. 268)
- ☐ Accommodation (p. 269)
- ☐ Compromise (p. 270)
- ☐ Team Mission (p. 234)
- ☐ Eight Criteria for Effective Mission Statements (p. 235)
- ☐ Mission Formulation (p. 236)
- ☐ Team Goals (p. 237)
- ☐ Goal Characteristics (p. 238)
- ☐ Stages of Team Development (p. 239)
- ☐ Forming Stage (p. 240)
- ☐ Storming Stage (p. 241)
- ☐ Norming Stage (p. 242)
- ☐ Performing Stage (p. 243)
- ☐ Team Member Roles (p. 244)
- ☐ Task Roles (p. 245)
- ☐ Process Roles (p. 246)
- ☐ Dysfunctional Team Member Behaviors (p. 247)
- ☐ Communication Process (p. 249)
- ☐ Task Communication (p. 251)
- ☐ Process Communication (p. 253)
- ☐ Communication Barriers (p. 254)
- ☐ Overcoming Communication Barriers (p. 255)
- ☐ The Difference Between Decision Making and Problem Solving (p. 259)
- ☐ Types of Decisions (p. 260)
- ☐ Decision-Making Procedures (p. 262)
- ☐ Problem-Solving Steps (p. 263)

- ☐ Conflict Management Strategies (p. 265)
- ☐ Steps to Managing Team Conflict (p. 271)
- ☐ Self-Authorized Team Leadership (p. 272)
- ☐ Behavioral Strategies (p. 273)
- ☐ Cognitive Strategies (p. 274)
- ☐ Increasing Leadership Effectiveness (p. 275)

Handouts

- ☐ Stages of Team Development (pp. 152-156)
- ☐ Team Member Roles (p. 158)
- ☐ Task Roles (p. 159)
- ☐ Process Roles (p. 160)
- ☐ Eight Criteria for Effective Mission Statements (p. 146)
- ☐ Team Mission (p. 147)
- ☐ Team Goals (p. 151)
- ☐ Dysfunctional Team Member Behaviors (p. 162)
- ☐ The Difference Between Decision Making and Problem Solving (p. 170)
- ☐ Types of Decisions (p. 171)
- ☐ Managing Team Conflict (p. 174)
- ☐ Conflict Management Strategies (p. 175)
- ☐ Conflict Resolutions (pp. 176-180)

Learning Activities

- ☐ Feedback Activity (pp. 202-204)

Tools and Assessments

- ☐ Team Development Rating Form (pp. 230-231)
- ☐ Leadership Role Checklist (pp. 228-229)
- ☐ Self-Authorized Team Leadership (p. 181)
- ☐ Behavioral Strategies (p. 182)
- ☐ Cognitive Strategies (p. 183)
- ☐ Increasing Leadership Effectiveness (pp. 184-186)
- ☐ Leadership Character (pp. 187-188)

Tailoring Tips

To tailor the workshop to your particular group, do the following:

- For ease in distributing and referring to materials in class, create a numbered handout packet. Bind or staple the packet.

- Design a custom cover with the name of the sponsoring organization, date, and place of the workshop, and print it on heavy paper (cover stock).

- Distribute the packet when you begin the workshop and refer participants to appropriate pages throughout the day.

Things to do

Prior to conducting the workshop, do the following:

Review Chapter 6: One-Day Teambuilding Worksho p

Refer to the overheads and handouts as you review the plans. Read the preparation section of each module and follow the instructions.

Prepare Materials

Photocopy the following:

- The workshop agenda and script. Write your planned start/stop times and anecdotal material on the photocopy.

- Participant handouts.

- Overheads

Tip: If you use transparency frames, you can make notes from the module content on the frame.

Prepare Flipcharts (see pp. 111-115)

- Sample mission statements and goals

- *Group Development Model*

- *Task and Process Involvement Model*

Inquire About Special Needs

Meet with the director of training and several of the individuals enrolled in the course to learn about any special needs, internal issues, and the experience level of participants.

Develop Relevant Examples

Develop examples that are relevant to the industry or enterprise.

Encourage Management Participation

Invite a middle or top manager to kick off the workshop and emphasize the important role supervisors play.

Suggested Flipcharts

1.

Group Development Models

Theories	Stage 1	Stage 2	Stage 3	Stage 4
Bennis Sheppard	Dependence	Counter-Dependence	Resolution	Inter-Dependence
Gibb	Acceptance	Data Flow	Goals and Norms	Control
Schutz	Inclusion	Control	Openness	Deinclusion
Tuckman	Forming	Storming	Norming	Performing
Kormanski Mozenter	Awareness	Conflict	Cooperation	Productivity
Varney	Formation	Building	Working	Maturity

2.

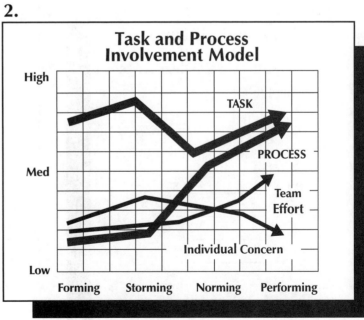

111

3.

Sample Mission Statements

We are the ABC team formed to provide quality information technology support to all customers, concentrating our resources on regional branches, and our efforts on exceeding customer expectations.

4.

Examples of Goals

(Record team observations here.)

5.

Goals and Missions

- Purpose
- Clarity
- Direction

- S _____
- M _____
- A _____
- R _____
- T _____

6.

Team Stages

(Record team observations here.)

7.

Stages of Team Development

Stages:

- Forming
- Norming
- Storming

8.

Examples of Roles

Task:

- Information giver
- Opinion giver
- Standard setter

Process:

- Encourager
- Gatekeeper
- Listener

9.

What Are Your Roles?

Roles:

(Record team observations here.)

10.

Task and Process Statements

Task:

- What?
- Why?
- I think that . . .

Process:

- How?
- I feel . . .

11.

Giving Feedback

- Reduces uncertainty.
- Solves problems.
- Builds trust.
- Strengthens relationships.
- Improves work quality.

12.

Examples of Problems

(Record team
observations here.)

13.

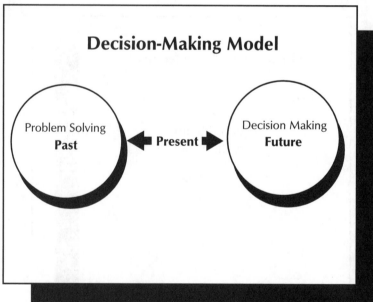

Decision-Making Model

Problem Solving
Past

◀ **Present** ▶

Decision Making
Future

14.

Team Problems

Problems:

(Record team
observations here.)

15.

Guidelines for Useful Feedback

- Be specific.
- Be descriptive.
- Be timely.
- Give ongoing feedback.

16.

Managing Conflict

- Personality.
- Values.
- Perspective.
- Goals.
- Culture.

17.

Leadership

Behavioral Strategies:

- Self-imposed outcomes.
- Self-management.
- Self-observation.
- Self-rewards.

Cognitive Strategies:

- Self-knowledge.
- Skill.
- Self-control.
- Purpose.

Training Plan

Team Purpose

Purpose   To examine the purpose of and the eight criteria for effective mission statements and the benefits and characteristics of team goals. This module may be used to develop, understand, and critique team mission statement and goals.

Objectives   After completion of this module, the participants will be able to:

- Describe the characteristics of a team mission statement.

- Use the criteria for effective team goals to develop or examine their goals.

Workshop Agenda

1. Team Purpose	Minutes 45	Start / Stop 8:00 / 8:45	Actual Start / Stop
Introduction	5	8:00 / 8:05	_____ / _____
Mission Statements • Criteria of Statements • Mission Formulation	15	8:05 / 8:20	_____ / _____
Goals • Team Goals • Goal Characteristics	10	8:20 / 8:30	_____ / _____
Group Discussion	10	8:30 / 8:40	_____ / _____
Key Points/Summary	5	8:40 / 8:45	_____ / _____

1. Team Purpose (8:00 to 8:45)

FACILITATOR COMMENTARY

00:05   **Introduction**

INTRODUCE the module and explain the purpose.

REVIEW the *Team Building Instrument* on *Team Purpose* to set the tone for what the team may need help with, based upon the survey results.

DISTRIBUTE the *Team Mission* handout (p. 147).

DEFINE team mission statements, using the *Team Mission* overhead (p. 234).

SHOW the overhead, *Eight Criteria for Effective Mission Statements* (p. 235), and ***DISTRIBUTE*** the handout (p. 146).

DESCRIBE the eight criteria of effective mission statements, using the background information in Chapter 2 (p. 16).

GROUP DISCUSSION

00:15   **Mission Statements**

SHOW sample mission statements on the flipchart.

ASK the group to review the statements and evaluate them according to the eight criteria.

DISCUSS the mission statements with the group, exploring what the impact might be on a group with a mission statement that does not meet the criteria.

ASK the class to identify the Who, What, and How in each mission statement.

DESCRIBE the three key components of effective mission statements, using the overhead, *Mission Formulation* (p. 236) and the information on page 17. Discuss the importance of these components in formulating a mission statement.

SUMMARIZE the purpose and importance of mission statements. Explain that the process of formulating an effective mission statement can take hours or days and is a separate activity.

FACILITATOR COMMENTARY

00:10   **Goals**

 SHOW the overhead, *Team Goals* (p. 237) and *DISTRIBUTE* the handout, *Team Goals* (p. 151).

DESCRIBE team goals, using page 20.

SHOW the overhead *Goal Characteristics* (p. 238).

DESCRIBE the five SMART characteristics for effective goals using page 21.

SHOW the flipchart, *Examples of Goals*.

LIST examples of different goals.

REVIEW the goals and evaluate them according to the SMART characteristics.

GROUP DISCUSSION

00:10   **Goals**

DISCUSS what the impact might be on a team that either does not have goals, or has poorly stated goals that do not include the five characteristics.

ASK how they might monitor the goals and what happens when the goals are met.

APPLY this information to the group. If they are an intact team, review their goals according to the criteria. If time allows, facilitate rewriting the goals so they conform to the characteristics. If participants do not have existing goals, facilitate developing a goal according to the characteristics.

POST the *Goals and Mission* flipcharts.

FACILITATOR COMMENTARY

00:05   **Key Points/Summary**

SUMMARIZE the purpose and importance of a clear team mission and sound goals, reviewing these key points.

- Mission statements guide teams toward their goals.

- Clear goals give the team a measurable path to take in achieving desired results.

- Teams without mission statements and clear goals will flounder and lose their effectiveness.

- Everyone's participation make these attainable.

Notes
- _____
- _____
- _____
- _____
- _____
- _____
- _____
- _____
- _____
- _____
- _____
- _____
- _____
- _____
- _____
- _____
- _____
- _____
- _____
- _____

Stages of Team Development

Purpose   This module explains the different stages of growth/change that a
                     team goes through, and how these stages affect the team output and
                     internal cohesion.

Objectives   After completion of this module, the participants will be able to
                     identify:

                     • Stages of team development.

                     • The current stage of the team.

Workshop Agenda

2. Stages of Team Development	Minutes 40	Start / Stop 8:45 / 9:25	Actual Start / Stop
Introduction	5	8:45 / 8:50	_____ / _____
Stages of Teams	5	8:50 / 8:55	_____ / _____
Characteristics of Stages • Forming • Storming • Norming • Performing	5	8:55 / 9:00	_____ / _____
Group Activity: Team Rating Form	10	9:00 / 9:10	_____ / _____
Group Discussion	10	9:10 / 9:20	_____ / _____
Key Points/Summary	5	9:20 / 9:25	_____ / _____
Break	10	9:25 / 9:35	_____ / _____

2. Stages of Team Development (8:45 to 9:25)

FACILITATOR COMMENTARY

00:05

Introduction

INTRODUCE the module and explain the purpose.

REVIEW the results from the *Team Building Instrument* on *Stages of Team Development*, to set the tone for what the team may need help with. Ask members to reflect on which stage they are in, based on the results of the survey.

00:05

Stages of Teams

DISTRIBUTE the handout, *Stages of Team Development* (p. 152).

DESCRIBE the stages of team development using the background information in Chapter 2 (p. 22) and the overhead (p. 239).

Note: These stages are based upon Tuckman's model for team development.

00:05

Characteristics of Stages

DISTRIBUTE the handouts, *Stage 1: Forming* (p. 153), *Stage 2: Storming* (p. 154), *Stage 3: Norming* (p. 155), and *Stage 4: Performing* (p.156).

DETAIL each stage using the background information from Chapter 2 (pp. 23-27), and the overheads (pp. 240-243).

DISCUSS examples of each stage.

WRITE team observations of stages on the flipchart, *Team Stages*.

ASK the following questions to generate discussion, or for thought starters.

- What stage does the team think they are in now?
- Why does the team think they are in this stage?
- What teams do you see that are stuck in certain stages?

DISCUSS any differences in the group, searching for agreement on the resolution of any differences that exist.

ADJUST the team observations on the flipchart to reflect group agreement.

POST the *Team Stages* flipchart.

GROUP ACTIVITY

00:10   **Team Development Rating**

DISTRIBUTE the *Team Development Rating Form* (p. 231) and refer to instructions on page 230.

GROUP DISCUSSION

00:10   **Group Discussion**

SHOW results of activity and *DISCUSS* the results with the entire team.

ASK the following questions to generate discussion, or for thought starters.

- Where does the team go from here?
- What do these scores mean?
- Is there any disagreement in the team now?
- How is work done in the team?
- What are your stages?

WRITE responses on the *Stages of Team Development* flipchart, under the heading "Stages."

FACILITATOR COMMENTARY

00:05   **Key Points/Summary**

SUMMARIZE these key points.

- All teams go through these stages.
- The stages are experienced in sequential order.
- New members will cause the team to start over.

00:10   **Break**

Team Member Roles

Purpose

In teams we see that team dynamics consist of task and process roles. Each member will, at certain times, play these roles. We will learn what will happen to a team if these roles are played but not at the right time, as well as when the roles are correctly played.

Objectives

After completion of this module, the participants will be able to:

- Identify and use the proper roles in their team structure.

- Explain the dynamics of interchangeable roles.

Workshop Agenda

3. Team Member Roles	Minutes 50	Start / Stop 9:35 / 10:25	Actual Start / Stop
Introduction	5	9:35 / 9:40	_____ / _____
Task/Process Model • Task Roles • Process Roles	10	9:40 / 9:50	_____ / _____
Group Activity: Role Identification	15	9:50 / 10:05	_____ / _____
Group Discussion	15	10:05 / 10:20	_____ / _____
Key Points/Summary	5	10:20 / 10:25	_____ / _____

3. Team Member Roles (9:35 to 10:25)

FACILITATOR COMMENTARY

00:05   **Introduction**

 INTRODUCE the module and explain the purpose.

REVIEW the *Team Member Roles* results from the *Team Building Instrument*. Ask members to reflect on the roles they play in their team as they review the survey results.

 DISTRIBUTE the handouts, *Team Member Roles* (p. 158), *Task Roles* (p. 159), and *Process Roles* (p. 160).

00:10   **Task Process Model**

 DESCRIBE and explain the Task/Process model using the overhead, *Team Member Roles* (p. 244). Distinguish between task and process.

 DESCRIBE the task roles using the background information in Chapter 2 (p. 30) and the overhead, *Task Roles* (p. 245).

 DESCRIBE the process roles using the background information in Chapter 2 (p. 31) and the overhead, *Process Roles* (p. 246).

 SHOW the flipchart, *Examples of Roles*.

 ASK for examples of different teams in the task and process roles, probing for several examples of each.

 WRITE team observations of the different roles members play on the flipchart.

ASK the following questions to generate discussion, or for thought starters.

- How does this correlate to what we found in the stages of team development?

- What is useful about being task focused?

- What is useful about being process focused?

- What are some disadvantages from being in one mode too frequently?

 POST the responses to the above questions on a flipchart.

GROUP ACTIVITY

00:15   **Role Identification**

ASK group members to identify three or four roles they have played recently or seen played by other team members.

EXPLAIN that each team member plays these roles at different times during a meeting. The purpose of this activity is to show how these roles shift.

SHOW the overhead, *Dysfunctional Team Member Behaviors* (p. 247) and *DISTRIBUTE* the handout (p. 162).

DESCRIBE dysfunctional behavior using the material in Chapter 2 (p. 33). Be careful not to personalize this issue. Ask how the team will deal with dysfunctional behavior when it does arise.

SHOW the overhead, *Responses to Dysfunctional Behavior* (p. 248) to describe.

GROUP DISCUSSION

00:15   **Role Identification**

ASK the following process learning questions:

- How will the team deal with the dysfunctional roles?
- How will the team deal with someone being too oriented to one style or the other?
- How will the team apply their knowledge so they may function better?

SHOW the flipchart, *What Are Your Roles?*

FACILITATOR COMMENTARY

00:05   **Key Points/Summary**

SUMMARIZE these key points.

- All teams have people in different roles at different times.
- Sometimes the roles are played dysfunctionally.
- Team members must have ways to deal with dysfunctional behaviors, or risk destroying the team.
- Team output is maximized by playing the correct roles at the correct times.

Team Communication

Purpose	Examine the critical importance of communication to effective teamwork, identifying strategies for improving the communication process.
Objectives	After completion of this module, the participants will be able to:

- Identify task and process language as indicators of team communication style.

- Identify barriers to the team's communication process.

- Practice strategies for giving and receiving feedback in order to improve team communication.

Prework	Read the background material in Chapter 2 on *Team Communication* (p. 35) . Refer to the overheads and handouts as you review the following. Prepare activity copies for participants.

 Note: Chapter 2 background information, *Stages of Team Development* (pp. 22-27) and *Team Member Roles* (pp. 29-32) provides information on task and process which link with this section. Actively build on these two.

Workshop Agenda

4. Team Communication	Minutes 60	Start / Stop 10:25 / 11:25	Actual Start / Stop
Introduction	5	10:25 / 10:30	_____ / _____
Communication Process • Task Communication • Process Communication • Barriers to Communication	20	10:30 / 10:50	
Group Activity • Giving Feedback • Receiving Feedback	15	10:50 / 11:05	_____ / _____
Group Discussion	15	11:05 / 11:20	_____ / _____
Key Points/Summary	5	11:20 / 11:25	_____ / _____
Lunch	60	11:25 / 12:55	_____ / _____

4. Team Communication (10:25 to 11:25)

FACILITATOR COMMENTARY

00:05   **Introduction**

INTRODUCE the module and explain the purpose. Emphasize that the quality of a team's work depends largely upon the quality of their information process.

REVIEW *Team Communication* in the *Team Building Instrument* (p. to set the tone for what the team may need help with, based on the survey results.

00:20   **Communication Process**

SHOW the overheads, *Communication Process* (p. 249), *Task Communication* (p. 250), and *Process Communication* (p. 252).

DESCRIBE the communication process, using the background material from Chapter 2 (pp. 35-36).

- Communication is exchange of information, which is transmitted, received, and acted upon.
- Sender must encode or translate thoughts into symbols.
- Message is sent verbally, electronically, or through writing.
- Receiver must decode or translate the message.
- When translation is accurate, effective communication occurs.
- Since people attach different meanings or translations, problems can occur.

ASK members to reflect on how effectively they are communicating and what is the stage of the team's development.

EXPLAIN that a team's language often reflects their state of development. Their communication can be characterized as task or process. A mismatch of process and task language can create miscommunication.

SHOW the overheads, *Task Communication is* . . .(p. 251) and *Process Communication is* . . .(p. 253).

DESCRIBE task and process communication, using the background material in Chapter 2 (pp. 37-38).

 ASK the group for examples of task and process statements, *WRITE* them on the flipchart and underline the key words. Have some of your own examples in mind, to stimulate the group if necessary. Guide the class in reviewing the statements and evaluating them according to the communication characteristics.

 SHOW the overhead, *Communication Barriers* (p. 254) and *DESCRIBE* barriers to communication, using page 39.

 SHOW the overhead, *Overcoming Communication Barriers* (p. 255) and *DESCRIBE* strategies for overcoming barriers, using page 41.

 DISCUSS how task and process statements can create barriers, depending on the receiver, and how to overcome them by different types of responses. Explore how understanding the two response types can enhance the team communication process.

 WRITE the responses on a flipchart.

 DESCRIBE giving and receiving feedback.

- Almost all aspects of team communication involve feedback.

- Smart members solicit feedback about their own behavior.

- Giving and receiving feedback effectively is a skill.

GROUP ACTIVITY

00:15   **Giving Feedback**

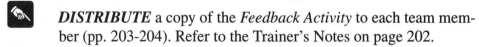 *EXPLAIN* the purpose of the activity: to explore guidelines for effective feedback to help the team strengthen their communication process.

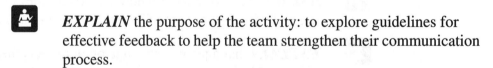 *DISTRIBUTE* a copy of the *Feedback Activity* to each team member (pp. 203-204). Refer to the Trainer's Notes on page 202.

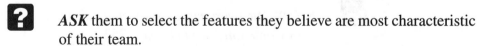 *ASK* them to select the features they believe are most characteristic of their team.

GROUP DISCUSSION

00:15   **Giving Feedback**

 FACILITATE a discussion, asking each member to relay his/her selections and explain how they describe the stage or effectiveness of the team.

 WRITE the responses on a flipchart.

- Prepare a simple matrix and note their key ideas by each feature.

- If time allows, discuss the notion of reasonable feedback— that which deals with behavior that can be changed by recipient.

(Optional) If time allows, continue the activity and discussion for *Receiving Feedback*. Conduct the activity and discussion the same as for *Giving Feedback*.

 DESCRIBE the guidelines for receiving feedback using page 42.

FACILITATOR COMMENTARY

00:05   **Key Points/Summary**

 SUMMARIZE the importance of effective team communication, making the following points about successful team members:

- They are aware of their language and its impact on others.

- They use validated techniques for giving and receiving feedback as a tool

  - for developing open channels of communication.

  - for enhancing the flexibility and performance of the team.

00:60   **Lunch**

Decision Making/Problem Solving

Purpose To understand the processes in which decisions are made and problems are solved. To better understand the difference between decision making and problem solving and what part these processes play in teams.

Objectives After completion of this module, the participants will be able to:

- Explain the difference between decision making and problem solving.

- Identify the proper process to use in the team.

Module Preparation Read Chapter 2 on *Making Decisions* and *Solving Problems* (pp. 46-51). Refer to the overheads for this module as you review the material. Prepare a flipchart with samples of the *Decision Making* model. Prepare handout copies for participants from the overheads, if desired.

Workshop Agenda

5. Decision Making/Problem Solving	Minutes 60	Start / Stop 12:25 / 1:25	Actual Start / Stop
Introduction	5	1:25 / 12:30	_____ / _____
Decision Making Model	5	12:30 / 12:35	_____ / _____
Characteristics of Decisions • Different Types of Decisions • Decision Model • Decision Making Procedures • Problem Solving Steps	15	12:35 / 12:50	_____ / _____
Group Activity: Problem Identification	15	12:50 / 1:05	_____ / _____
Group Discussion	15	1:05 / 1:20	_____ / _____
Key Points/Summary	5	1:20 / 1:25	_____ / _____

5. Decision Making/Problem Solving (12:25 to 1:25)

FACILITATOR COMMENTARY

00:05   **Introduction**

INTRODUCE the module and explain the purpose.

REVIEW the *Team Processes* results from the *Team Building Instrument* to set the tone for what the team may need help with. Ask members to reflect on how effectively they make decisions or solve problems.

00:05   **Decision-Making Model**

SHOW the overhead *The Difference Between Decision Making and Problem Solving* (p. 259) and *DISTRIBUTE* the handout (p. 170).

DESCRIBE the difference of these two processes using (p. 46). Emphasize these two points:

- Decision-making process is anchored in the future.
- Problem-solving process deals with events in the past.

00:15   **Characteristics of Decisions**

SHOW the overhead *Types of Decisions* (p. 260) and *DISTRIBUTE* the handout (p. 171).

EXPLAIN the different types of decisions using page 47. Explore the four types of decision making.

- Complex Decisions
- Yes-and-No Decisions
- Single-Course-of-Action Decisions
- One-Alternative Decisions

DISCUSS what these decision types mean to the team and how to choose the most appropriate one to use.

DESCRIBE decision-making procedures using pages 48-49.

DESCRIBE the problem-solving steps using pages 50-51.

ASK the following questions to generate discussion, or for thought starters.

- Why is the decision-making process focused in the future?
- Why is there confusion about these two processes?
- When is it okay to change decision-making types?
- When is it not okay to change decision-making types?

GROUP ACTIVITY

00:15   **Problem Identification**

EXPLAIN the purpose of the activity.

ASK participants to select a problem currently affecting the team. Go through the *Problem-Solving Steps* using page 50 and the overhead, *Problem Solving Steps* (p. 263).

After determining the desired future state (problem solved) *USE* the *Decision-Making Methods* on page 40 and the overhead, *Decision-Making Procedures* (p. 262) to decide how best to implement the change plan that will keep the problem from recurring.

EXPLAIN that each team member may view the problems differently. Still, try to agree on three or four problems and select one to solve. This is the identify stage; do not get too far ahead of the steps. Move through the problem-solving model to solve the selected problem. Develop an evaluation plan to monitor progress and to determine if the problem is solved or not.

SHOW the flipchart, *Examples of Problems*. Use the flipchart to list different problems that team members are aware of and write their responses on the flipchart.

GROUP DISCUSSION

00:15   **Process Learning**

ASK the following process learning questions:

*   How was the activity using the new processes?

*   What are the benefits of using these processes?

*   What does the team do now for decision-making and problem-solving processes?

*   What are the predominant types of decisions the team will be making?

RECORD responses on the *Team Problems* flipchart, under the heading "Problems".

FACILITATOR COMMENTARY

00:05 **Key Points/Summary**

SUMMARIZE the module with these key points.

- Decision making and problem solving are different processes.
- You can do the processes independently of each other.
- Teams should have the skills to do both equally effectively.

Notes

- _____
- _____
- _____
- _____
- _____
- _____
- _____
- _____
- _____
- _____
- _____
- _____
- _____
- _____
- _____
- _____
- _____
- _____
- _____
- _____
- _____
- _____
- _____
- _____

Managing Team Conflict

Purpose   Explore the causes of team conflict and five strategies for managing conflict.

Objectives   After completion of this module, the participants will be able to:

- Determine the source of conflict that arises in teams.
- Practice strategies for dealing with team conflict.

Workshop Agenda

6. Managing Team Conflict	Minutes 1 hr 5	Start / Stop 1:25 / 2:45	Actual Start / Stop
Introduction	5	1:25 / 1:30	____ / ____
Causes of Conflict	5	1:30 / 1:35	____ / ____
Conflict Management Strategies • Competition • Collaboration • Avoidance • Accommodation • Compromise	20	1:35 / 1:55	____ / ____
Group Activity: Conflict Resolution	15	1:55 / 2:10	____ / ____
Group Discussion: Conflict Resolution	15	2:10 / 2:25	____ / ____
Key Points/Summary	5	2:25 / 2:30	____ / ____
Break	15	2:30 / 2:45	____ / ____

6. Managing Team Conflict (1:25 to 2:45)

FACILITATOR COMMENTARY

00:05   **Introduction**

INTRODUCE the module and explain the purpose. Emphasize that the quality of a team's work depends largely upon the quality of their information process.

EMPHASIZE that the ability to resolve team conflict is the most important skill team members can develop

REVIEW the results from the *Team Building Instrument* to set the tone for what the team may need help with, based on the survey results. Ask members to reflect on how effectively they are managing conflict, based on the results of the survey.

00:05   **Causes of Conflict**

SHOW the overhead *Causes of Team Conflict* (p. 264).

ASK participants to name possible sources of team conflict and lead into describing these five causes:

*   Personality differences
*   Values differences
*   Differences in perspective
*   Differences in goals
*   Cultural differences

GROUP DISCUSSION

00:20   **Conflict Management Strategies**

DISCUSS team members' perspectives of the causes, and how their conflict is a result of these causes.

LINK the stage of the team's development and how this may be reflected in their team conflict temperature. (Storming usually involves considerable conflict).

DISTRIBUTE the handouts, *Managing Team Conflict* (p. 174) and *Conflict Managment Strategies* (p. 175), and *EXPLAIN* that conflict is natural, but resolving it is a skil. Use the background material in Chapter 2 (p. 53) and the overhead, *Conflict Management Strategies* (p. 265) as a transition into the five strategies for managing conflict.

SHOW the overheads *Competition* (p. 266), *Collaboration* (p. 267), *Avoidance* (p. 268), *Accommodation* (p. 269), and *Compromise* (p. 270) and *DISTRIBUTE* the handouts (pp. 176-180).

DETAIL each strategy:

- Competition
- Collaboration
- Avoidance
- Accommodation
- Compromise

ASK the group to name situations of conflict present in the team.

WRITE the responses on the flipchart.

ASK the group to review the situations and determine which strategy is most appropriate in each situation.

REVIEW the overhead that summarizes each strategy.

DESCRIBE the steps to manage team conflict, as a possible model for the team, using page 53. Transition to the activity as a way for the team to practice the steps.

GROUP ACTIVITY

00:15   **Conflict Resolution**

EXPLAIN the purpose of the activity: to practice managing conflict, and to help the team strengthen their skills.

SHOW the overhead, *Steps to Managing Team Conflict* (p. 271) for reference.

Remind them to use the guidelines for useful feedback (pp. 203-204).

Select an actual team conflict situation from the list generated earlier. Guide the group through the steps.

WRITE the outcomes to each step on the flipchart.

Identify which conflict management strategy would be most appropriate in this situation.

GROUP DISCUSSION

00:15   **Conflict Resolution**

 DISCUSS and review the posted information with the team members.

- How did it go? What worked? What could be improved in their application of the model?

- Did their selected conflict strategy apply to the situation? How does the strategy reflect their teams current stage of development?

- How will they implement the solution?

- How can they remember to apply this management system with future conflicts?

 POST the *Managing Conflict* flipchart.

FACILITATOR COMMENTARY

00:05   **Key Points/Summary**

 MAKE these key points to summarize the benefits of successfully using team conflicts.

- Conflict is useful when viewed as an opportunity for discussing and managing problems, which are inevitable in human relationships.

- The quality of decision making can be improved by allowing different points of view to be examined.

- Conflict is healthy when effectively managed. It is an antidote for "group think." It does not allow the team to passively accept decisions that may be based on incomplete or inappropriate information. It challenges the status quo and facilitates the consideration of new ideas.

00:15   **Break**

Self-Authorized Team Leadership

Purpose   To understand the role of self-leadership in the team and how to improve team roles.

Objectives   After completion of this module, the participants will be able to emulate the characteristics of self-leadership.

Workshop Agenda

7. Self-Authorized Team Leadership	Minutes 60	Start / Stop 2:45 / 3:45	Actual Start / Stop
Introduction	5	2:45 / 2:50	_____ / _____
Self-Authorized Team Leadership	5	2:50 / 2:55	_____ / _____
Strategies • Behavioral • Cognitive • Increasing Leadership Effectiveness • Seven Pillars of Leadership	15	2:55 / 3:10	_____ / _____
Group Activity: • Leadership Role Checklist	15	3:10 / 3:25	_____ / _____
Group Discussion	15	3:25 / 3:40	_____ / _____
Key Points/Summary	5	3:40 / 3:45	_____ / _____

7. Self-Authorized Team Leadership (2:45 to 3:45)

FACILITATOR COMMENTARY

00:05 **Introduction**

INTRODUCE the module, explaining the purpose.

REVIEW the *Team Leadership* results from the *Team Building Instrument*. Ask members to reflect on how effectively the team uses leadership, based on the survey results.

00:05 **Self-Authorized Team Leadership**

SHOW the overhead, *Self-Authorized Team Leadership* (p. 272) and ***DISTRIBUTE*** the handout (p. 181).

DESCRIBE the team leadership that is focused on self, using the background material in Chapter 2 (p. 57). Emphasize these basic assumptions:

- Everyone practices self-leadership to some degree.
- Self-leadership is applicable to everyone.
- Not everyone is an effective self-leader.
- Self-leadership skills can be developed.

00:15 **Strategies**

SHOW the overheads, *Behavioral Strategies* (p. 273) and *Cognitive Strategies* (p. 274) and ***DISTRIBUTE*** the handouts (pp. 182-183).

DETAIL the four basic assumptions of the two basic types of leadership strategies, using pages 57-58. Note the difference between these two types.

- Behavioral strategies are self-directed outcomes.
- Cognitive strategies focus on the aspects of teamwork.

SHOW the overhead, *Increasing Leadership Effectiveness* (p. 276) and ***DISTRIBUTE*** the handouts (pp. 184-186).

DISCUSS the four points for increasing leadership effectiveness using page 59.

SHOW the overhead, *The Seven Pillars of Leadership Character* (p. 276) and ***DISTRIBUTE*** the handouts (pp. 187-188).

DISCUSS *The Seven Pillars of Leadership Character* (p. 60), asking what these do for a leader.

ASK the following questions to generate discussion, or for thought starters.

- Why is self-leadership important to teams?
- Does everyone have to be a leader?
- What would happen if everyone tried to lead?
- What would happen if no one led?
- What happens when one person always leads?

USE the flipchart to list responses that team members share on their views of leadership and ***POST*** the flipchart.

GROUP ACTIVITY

00:15   **Leadership Role Checklist**

DISTRIBUTE copies of the *Leadership Role Checklist* (p. 229). Emphasize that this will only give the team a snapshot of the leadership strategy that they employ on a daily basis.

TABULATE responses from the group.

WRITE responses on a flipchart.

EXPLAIN that these responses can lead to significant improvement in how members work inside and outside the team.

GROUP DISCUSSION

00:15   **Leadership Roles**

DISCUSS results from the checklist. Does the team recognize any knowledge gained from the results?

ASK the following questions to generate discussion, or for thought starters.

- What does this say about the team?
- Does the team, in fact, share leadership roles?
- How can the team improve the sharing of leadership?
- How can the team promote self-leadership?
- How can the team move more effectively in this direction?

RECORD responses on the *Leadership* flipchart, under the heading "Leadership."

FACILITATOR COMMENTARY

00:05

Key Points/Summary

SUMMARIZE these key points.

- Self-authorized leadership is something that each member is capable of.

- Self-leadership starts inside each member.

- There are strategies we can use to improve our leadership abilities.

- The team will become more effective as each member becomes a better leader.

Notes

- _____

- _____

- _____

- _____

- _____

- _____

- _____

- _____

- _____

- _____

- _____

- _____

- _____

- _____

- _____

- _____

- _____

- _____

- _____

Chapter Seven:

Participant Handouts

In this section, you will find participant handouts for use during your teambuilding training.

USING HANDOUT MASTERS

You may use the handout masters in two ways :

- Key them into your word processing system "as is" or customize them to suit your specific needs.

- Photocopy the masters that you need from this book and use them "as is."

This chapter also contains the following additional handouts to enhance your teambuilding training program:

- *Reasons for Teambuilding* (p. 144)

- *Effective Team Characteristics* (p. 145)

- *Team Purpose* (p. 146)

- *Writing a Mission Statement* (p. 148)

- *Team Mission: Who? What? and How?* (p. 149)

- *Operating Principles or the "How"* (p. 150)

- *Theories of Group Development* (p. 157)

- *Task and Process Involvement* (p. 161)

- *Team Communication* (pp. 163-166)

- *Decision-Making Procedures* (p. 172)

- *Problem Solving* (p. 173)

Reasons for Teambuilding

Read the following reasons for teambuilding and consider what information you will need to become a more effective team member.

1. **To establish team purpose.**

    I know the purpose of my team.   Yes: _____ No: _____

    If no, what do I need to find out?

    _____

    _____

2. **To understand the stages of team development.**

    I understand team stages.   Yes: _____ No: _____

    If no, what do I need to find out?

    _____

    _____

3. **To analyze how the team works based on team member roles.**

    I understand team member roles.   Yes: _____ No: _____

    If no, what do I need to find out?

    _____

    _____

4. **To develop effective team communication.**

    I understand effective team communication. Yes: _____ No: _____

    If no, what do I need to find out?

    _____

    _____

5. **To examine team processes.**

    I understand team process.   Yes: _____ No: _____

    If no, what do I need to find out?

    _____

    _____

6. **To understand team leadership.**

    I understand the meaning of team
    leadership.   Yes: _____ No: _____

    If no, what do I need to find out?

    _____

    _____

Effective Team Characteristics

Effective team characteristics are important to know and understand. Some characteristics of effective teams are as follows:

Team members:

- Share a common identity.

- Have common goals and objectives.

- Share common leadership.

- Share successes and failures.

- Cooperate and collaborate.

- Have membership roles.

Teams:

- Are comprised of diverse people.

- Make decisions effectively.

Team Purpose

A team's purpose is defined by its mission. A team's mission is defined as something that the team intends to do. It is the object for which the team exists as determined by the team leader and team members. It is a clearly stated purpose that serves to direct and motivate the team in its pursuit of its goals.

Eight Criteria for Effective Mission Statements

1. Inspirational.

2. Clear and challenging.

3. Differentiating.

4. Stable but constantly challenging.

5. Beacons and controls.

6. Empowering.

7. Future oriented.

8. Clear and concise.

Team Mission

Effective teams are driven by an inspiring mission that must support the organization's vision. The mission is best expressed in written format stating the team's intended direction.

A clearly articulated mission provides the foundation for developing goals and action plans that will assist the team in reaching its desired outcomes. The mission statement must contain three key elements:

- What does the team do?
- For whom does the team perform its functions?
- How does the team go about doing its job?

Formulate your mission statement:

1. **What does your team do?**

_____

_____

_____

_____

2. **For whom do you perform your function?**

_____

_____

_____

_____

_____

3. **How does your team go about doing the work?**

_____

_____

_____

_____

_____

Writing a Mission Statement

What does the team do?

This element defines the purpose of the team. It specifies what the team does, the nature of the team's business, and why the team exists. It must be determined unanimously by all team members, otherwise the team will unravel and eventually fall apart.

For whom does the team perform the function?

This element defines who the primary customer is that the team serves. It identifies who will receive the benefits of the team's output. There should be interaction with the identified customer and discussion about how the team can meet the customer's needs.

Sample mission statement

> ## THE ABC TEAM
>
> We are the ABC team formed to provide quality information technology support to all customers, concentrating our resources on regional branches, and our efforts on exceed-ing customer expectations.

Team Mission: Who? What? and How?

The mission statement is a combination of specific facts that are integrated with parts of the organization's vision. It must be realistic and in line with the organization's resources and personnel. It must be compelling and attainable. An unrealistic mission statement that cannot be acted upon only serves to undermine morale and team leadership.

Operating Principles or the "How"

Operating principles are the foundation of how team members get things done. They are based on stated values that guide the way team members work with each other. They are determined by examining individual values in relation to other team member values. This examination of values contributes to the establishment of a set of team stated principles that will serve to guide how the team operates on a day-to-day basis.

List five important values that motivate you to do your best work:

1. _____

   _____

2. _____

   _____

3. _____

   _____

4. _____

   _____

5. _____

   _____

Compare your list with other members of your team. Are there any similarities? Are there any differences?

The team's operating principles must be in alignment with organizational values that drive the way the business is accomplished.

Team Goals

A team goal is an end that the team strives to reach.

- It supports the mission.
- It supports the organization's vision.

Common goals provide team member with . . .

Purpose   What needs to be done.

Clarity   What the outcome looks like.

Direction   The path to be followed.

To be effective, goals must have the following characteristics:

S   **Specific**

M   **Measurable**

A   **Attainable**

R   **Relevant**

T   **Time Bound**

Stages of Team Development

When a group of people are first formed into a team, their roles and interactions are not established. Some individuals may merely act as observers while they try to determine what is expected from them while others may engage the process immediately.

There are many models that describe team developmental progression. They are similar and suggest that the process occurs in four predictable stages.

Each stage is characteristically different and builds on the preceding one. The implication is that all teams must develop through this predetermined sequence if they are to be fully functioning teams.

Four Stages of Team Development

Stage 1:   **Forming**

Stage 2:   **Storming**

Stage 3:   **Norming**

Stage 4:   **Performing**

Stage 1: Forming

The Forming stage of team development is an exploration period. Team members are often cautious and guarded in their interactions not really knowing what to expect from other team members.

- They explore the boundaries of acceptable behavior.

- Behaviors expressed in this early stage are generally polite and noncommittal.

Some questions raised during this stage of development are:

- Do I want to be part of this team?

- Will I be accepted as a member?

- Who is the leader?

- Is the leader competent?

Participant response

When you were a member of a team that worked well together, what is your recollection of the Forming stage?

_____

_____

_____

_____

_____

_____

_____

_____

_____

_____

_____

_____

_____

_____

_____

Stage 2: Storming

The Storming stage of development is characterized by competition and strained relationships among team members. There are various degrees of conflict that teams experience but basically the Storming stage deals with issues of power, leadership, and decision making.

- Conflict cannot be avoided during this stage.

- It is the most crucial stage the team must work through.

Some questions raised during this stage of development are:

- How will I seek my autonomy?

- How much control will I have over others?

- Who do I support?

- Who supports me?

- How much influence do I have?

Participant response

When you were a member of a team that worked well together, what is your recollection of the Storming stage?

_____

_____

_____

_____

_____

_____

_____

_____

_____

_____

_____

_____

_____

_____

Stage 3: Norming

The Norming stage of team development is characterized by cohesiveness among team members. After working through the Storming stage, team members discover that they in fact do have common interests with each other.

- They learn to appreciate their differences.

- They work better together.

- They problem solve together.

Some questions raised during this stage of development are:

- What kind of relationships can we develop?

- Will we be successful as a team?

- How do we measure up to other teams?

- What is my relationship to the team leader?

Participant response

When you were a member of a team that worked well together, what is your recollection of the Norming stage?

_____

_____

_____

_____

_____

_____

_____

_____

_____

_____

_____

_____

_____

_____

_____

Stage 4: Performing

The Performing stage of team development is the result of working through the first three stages. By this time, team members have learned how to work together as a fully functioning team.

- They can define tasks.

- They can work out their relationships successfully.

- They can manage their conflicts.

- The can work together to accomplish their mission.

Participant response

When you were a member of a team that worked well together, what is your recollection of the Performing stage?

_____

_____

_____

_____

_____

_____

_____

_____

_____

_____

_____

_____

_____

_____

_____

_____

_____

_____

_____

Theories of Group Development

The Tuckman Model[1] (forming, storming, norming, and performing) is generally accepted as the basic model of team development. It incorporates many aspects of the theories considered in this discussion and has remained relatively constant since it was introduced.

Theorists	Stage 1	Stage 2	Stage 3	Stage 4
Bennis Sheppard	Dependence	Counter-Dependence	Resolution	Inter-Dependence
Gibb	Acceptance	Data Flow	Goals and Norms	Control
Schutz	Inclusion	Control	Openness	Deinclusion
Tuckman	Forming	Storming	Norming	Performing
Kormanski Mozenter	Awareness	Conflict	Cooperation	Productivity
Varney	Formation	Building	Working	Maturity

1. *Team Building* by Reddy, W. and Jamison, K. 1988. San Diego, CA: NTL and University Associates.

Team Member Roles

When individuals come together to form a team, a number of dynamics occur simultaneously.

- Some members are goal oriented.

- Others spend more time working on interpersonal issues.

As team development progresses, members settle into individual "roles" by mutual consent.

- These roles include both "task" and "process" areas.

- The task dynamic is identified by the "what" and "why" issues of the team's work.

- The process dynamic is the "how" dynamic that the team uses to facilitate task accomplishment.

    Task = "What" and "Why"

    Process = "How"

Task Roles

Task roles include:

- Establishing the mission.

- Determining operating principles.

- Setting goals.

- Establishing team member roles.

Some task roles played by team members are as follows:

Information giver	Offers authoritative information or data.
Information seeker	Asks for clarification or accuracy of statements.
Initiator	Makes suggestions or proposes new ideas.
Opinion giver	States belief or opinions relative to the discussion.
Elaborator	Elaborates on ideas and suggestions, defines and redefines terms.
Consensus seeker	Polls the group for its readiness to make decisions or resolve conflicts.
Clarifier	Interprets or explains facts or opinions.
Standard setter	Establishes criteria for evaluating opinions, ideas, or decisions.
Representative	Reports the team's progress or actions outside the team.

Participant response

What "task" roles do you find yourself playing when you are a member of a team?

_____

_____

_____

_____

_____

_____

_____

_____

Process Roles

Process roles focus on:

- The team's needs for commitment, dependence, and involvement.

- Factors such as which team members talk, and who talks to whom.

Some process role qualities displayed by team members are:

Encouraging	Being open to others' opinions or feelings even if they are different.
Gatekeeping	Openly taking interest in what others say, and facilitating communication.
Listening	Paying close attention to what others talk about.
Harmonizing	Negotiating or relieving tension when appropriate.
Yielding	Giving up an unpopular viewpoint and admitting mistakes.
Accepting	Respecting and promoting differences.
Supporting	Giving team members permission to feel good about their successes.

Participant response

What "process" roles do you find yourself playing when you are a member of a team?

_____

_____

_____

_____

_____

_____

_____

_____

_____

_____

Task and Process Involvement

Task roles have a tendency to dominate during the early stages of the teams development whereas process roles increase in their importance during the later stages of the process.

As the team matures, task and process roles parallel each other in their importance, which contributes to the effective functioning of the team. Individual contribution subordinates itself to team effort.

The team must acquire a balance of task and process functions if it is to realize its potential as a fully functioning team.

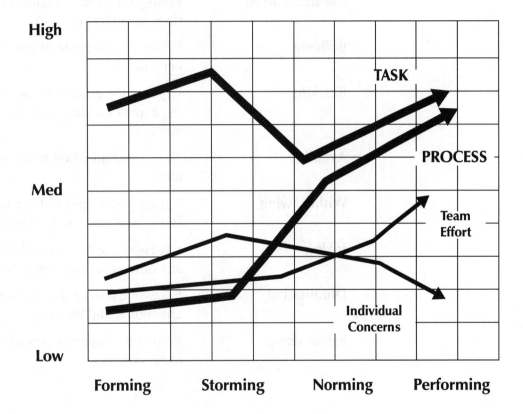

Dysfunctional Team Member Behaviors

Dysfunctional team member behaviors can impact the work flow of the team if not appropriately challenged.

- Some task behaviors can interfere with the team being able to accomplish its goal.
- Some process behaviors can prevent the team from developing a supportive climate.

Some of the dysfunctional task behaviors are as follows:

Condescending	Putting down team member contributions as irrelevant.
Bullying	Being inconsiderate of other team member's needs.
Blocking	Arguing too much on a point and rejecting expressed ideas without consideration.
Avoiding	Not paying attention to facts or relevant ideas.
Withdrawing	Acting passive or indifferent, wandering from the subject of discussion.
Joking	Excessive playing around, telling jokes, and mimicking other members.
Dominating	Excessive talking, interrupting others, criticizing, and blaming.
Self-Seeking	Putting one's personal needs before the team's needs.

Team Communication

Team communication is defined as the exchange of information between team members that is satisfactorily transmitted, received, and acted upon.

- Communication includes the transference and understanding of meaning between the sender and the receiver.

- An idea, regardless of its value, is just an idea until other team members understand it.

- The quality of the team's work, to a large extent, depends upon the quality of information they share.

The Process of Communication

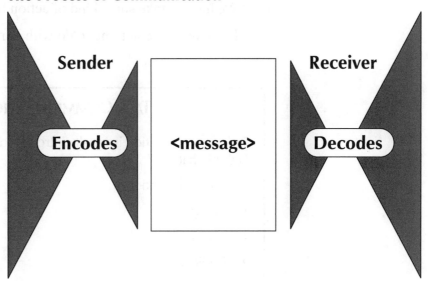

Sender — Encodes — <message> — Receiver — Decodes

Task Communication

Task communication is "head talk" that leads to the explanation of the team situation. It is bound by rules of logic that may or may not be true.

• A task statement can be proven or disproven. Words must be communicated in order to produce task statements. The statement, "I think that . . ." is indicative of the speaker using task communication. Task communication is analytical, linear, explicit, verbal, auditory, concrete, active, and adaptive.

• Some task statements that team members make are:

"Our purpose is solely to achieve the mission."

"We have to take some kind of action immediately."

"Emotions have nothing to do with our work."

TASK COMMUNICATION

Task communication is usually introduced by the statement, "I think that . . ."

Task communication is:

• Analytical.

• Linear.

• Explicit.

• Verbal.

• Auditory.

• Concrete.

• Active.

Process Communication

Process communication is "gut" talk that leads to an understanding of the team situation. It explains an individual's internal, affective, nonrational response.

- Process statements are usually personal in nature and refer to the individual's state of being.

- They are neither good or bad, nor true or false.

- Some common statements made in tense discussions are "Now, let's not get personal," or "Let's just stick to the work and not let our feelings interfere with it."

- When process statements are made, the form is usually stated as "I feel . . ." (adjective) or "I feel . . ." (adverb).

- Process communication is intuitive, spontaneous, emotional, visual, artistic, playful, and innovative.

- "Synergy is the outcome of our team process."

PROCESS COMMUNICATION

Process communication is usually introduced by the stat e-ment, "I feel . . ."

Process communication is:

- Intuitive.

- Spontaneous.

- Emotional.

- Visual.

- Artistic.

- Playful.

Barriers to Effective
Team Communication

Barriers in team communication result from the inability of team members to distinguish the difference between various communication channels we use to speak, such as facts, individuals feelings, personal values, and opinions.

Facts   A fact is something that has actually happened or that is really true without any emotional reference.

Feelings   Feelings refer to any subjective reaction, pleasurable or unpleasurable, that a person may have to a situation, sometimes with the absence of reason.

Values   Values refer to important personal ideals that make people behave the way they do.

Opinions   Opinions are a set of beliefs not based on absolute certainty but on what seems true to one's own mind.

Giving Feedback

Almost all aspects of team communication involve feedback—giving and receiving information about team-related performance.

By giving clear and concise feedback, team members and the entire organization will benefit. Some benefits of giving feedback are as follows:

BENEFITS OF GIVING FEEDBACK

- Feedback reduces uncertainty.

- Feedback solves problems.

- Feedback builds trust.

- Feedback can strengthen relationships.

- Feedback improves work quality.

Giving Feedback to Others

Giving feedback is a verbal or nonverbal process in which a team member shares his or her feelings or perceptions about another team member's behavior or actions.

The process of giving and receiving feedback is one of the most important ways for learning new behaviors and determining the impact of our behavior on others.

Some guidelines for giving feedback are as follows:

1. Feedback should be specific.

2. Be descriptive, not evaluative with feedback.

3. Be timely with the feedback.

4. Feedback must be on-going.

Receiving Feedback from Others

There should be reciprocity in feedback. If team members can give feedback, they should be able to receive feedback. When soliciting feedback from others, it is helpful to follow these guidelines:

RECEIVING FEEDBACK FROM OTHERS

- Get as much information as possible.
- Do not become defensive.
- Use the feedback you solicit.

Giving and receiving feedback are two important parts of effective team communication. The guidelines presented will assist team members in developing open channels of communication where team members can learn and grow from each other.

Decision Making

Decision making is a process by which team members arrive at a decision, judgment, or conclusion through a process of deliberation.

• It is one of the most critical applications of teamwork.

• We all have to make decisions.

The Difference Between Decision Making and Problem Solving

Decision making and problem solving are two different types of team processes that require two very different methods for accomplishing their outcomes.

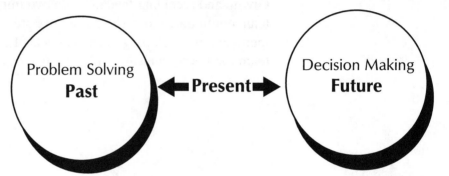

Problem Solving	Problem solving has its origins in the past. A problem is something that has gone wrong in the past and must be managed in the present. It is more precise and objective than decision making.
Decision Making	Decision making is rooted in the present with a look into the future for resolution. A decision is a commitment to a course of action selected from several alternatives.

Types of Decisions

When considering possible courses of action, team members must evaluate the objectives, alternatives, and potential risks of their decision. Decisions can be classified into these four categories:

1. **Complex decisions.**

   Complex decisions require large amounts of information and involvement by all team members.

2. **Yes-and-no decisions.**

   Yes-and-no decisions involve two alternatives either to accept or reject the proposal.

3. **Single-course-of-action decisions.**

   Single-course-of-action decisions involve determining whether the proposed measure should be implemented.

4. **One-alternative decisions.**

   One-alternative decisions are concerned with whether a measure should be adopted.

Decision-Making Procedures

The five decision-making procedures that facilitate team decision-making are:

1. **Decision by authority.**

    Decision by authority occurs when the highest ranking authority within the team, usually the appointed team leader or manager, makes a unilateral decision.

2. **Decision by minority.**

    Decision by minority occurs when a small group of team members exert their influence over the majority of the team.

3. **The democratic process.**

    The democratic process of decision making occurs when a majority of team members agree with the issues.

4. **Decision by consensus.**

    Decision by consensus means finding a proposal that is acceptable enough so that all team members can support it.

5. **Decision by unanimity.**

    Decision by unanimity occurs when all team members are in full agreement with the decision. This procedure is often confused with consensus decision-making. The team should make unanimous decisions when the team issues are important and effect all team members.

Problem Solving

One of the primary responsibilities of team membership is the ability to solve problems that impact the team.

- To be effective, team members must be able to identify problems and have a desire to resolve them.

- Trying to solve a problem without a systematic process is like trying to find your way in the wilderness without a good topographical map.

Problem-Solving Steps

1. Define the problem.

2. Identify the desired future state.

3. Identify the forces promoting change and the forces restraining change.

4. Analyze forces that can be changed.

5. Plan a change strategy.

6. Develop an action plan.

7. Evaluate your actions.

Managing Team Conflict

Conflict is a daily reality for all team members. Team members' needs and values inevitably come into conflict with the needs and values of others.

- Some of the conflicts are minor and can be managed easily while others have a greater intensity and require a strategy for effective resolution.

- The ability to resolve team conflict is the most important skill that team members can develop.

Causes of Team Conflict

1. Personality differences.

2. Difference in values.

3. Difference in perspective.

4. Difference in goals.

5. Cultural differences.

Conflict Management Strategies

Conflict situations are situations in which the needs, wants, or values of team members clash.

- As a result of this clash, team members can react to the conflict in five basic ways.

- They either compete, collaborate, avoid, accommodate, or compromise with one another.

Competition	Competition is characterized by the need to win at all costs. It is a win-lose situation with the need to dominate.
Collaboration	Collaboration is characterized by a desire to satisfy all team members in a win-win situation.
Avoidance	Avoidance is characterized by attempts to distract attention from the issue or ignore it completely.
Accommodation	Accommodation is characterized by the desire to please others at the expense of a person's own needs.
Compromise	Compromise is described by meeting the conflict at midpoint. Both parties in a dispute achieve moderate but incomplete satisfaction.

When to Use the Conflict Strategies

Using the appropriate conflict strategy is important when managing conflict situations. It is meaningful to acknowledge which conflict resolution approach is being used and the situation in which it can be used most effectively.

Conflict resolution: Competition

COMPETITION

Competition is appropriate when:

- Quick, decisive action is necessary.
- The issues are important and unpopular actions need to be implemented.
- The issues are vital to the team's welfare and you know you are right.
- When dealing with people who take advantage of non-competitive behavior.
- Other options are not possible.

Notes

- _____
- _____
- _____
- _____
- _____
- _____
- _____
- _____
- _____
- _____
- _____
- _____
- _____
- _____
- _____
- _____
- _____
- _____

**Conflict resolution:
  Collaboration**

COLLABORATION

Collaboration is appropriate when:

- You need to find an integrative solution and both sets of concerns are too important to be compromised.

- Your objective is to learn.

- You need to merge insights from people with different perspectives.

- You want to gain commitment by incorporating concerns into a consensus decision.

- You want to work through feelings that have interfered with a relationship.

Notes

- _____
- _____
- _____
- _____
- _____
- _____
- _____
- _____
- _____
- _____
- _____
- _____
- _____
- _____
- _____
- _____
- _____
- _____
- _____

Conflict resolution:
Avoidance

AVOIDANCE

Avoidance is appropriate when:

- An issue is trivial or more important issues are pressing.
- You see that there is no chance to satisfy your major concerns.
- You need to let people cool down and regain perspective.
- You need more time to gather information.
- Others can resolve the conflict more effectively.

Notes

- _____
- _____
- _____
- _____
- _____
- _____
- _____
- _____
- _____
- _____
- _____
- _____
- _____
- _____
- _____
- _____
- _____
- _____
- _____
- _____
- _____
- _____

Conflict resolution:
Accommodation

ACCOMMODATION

Accommodation is appropriate when:

- You find that you are wrong.
- You want to show your reasonableness.
- Issues are more important to others than yourself.
- You want to build social support for later use.
- You want to minimize your losses.
- You want to allow other team members to develop by learning from mistakes.

Notes

- _____
- _____
- _____
- _____
- _____
- _____
- _____
- _____
- _____
- _____
- _____
- _____
- _____
- _____
- _____
- _____
- _____
- _____
- _____

Conflict resolution: Compromise

COMPROMISE

Compromise is appropriate when :

*   Goals are important but not worth the effort of disru p- tion.
*   Opponents with equal power are committed to different means to a similar end.
*   You want to achieve temporary settlements to complex issues.
*   You want to strive at an expedient solution under time pressure.
*   You need backup because collaboration or competition is not working.

Notes

*   _____
*   _____
*   _____
*   _____
*   _____
*   _____
*   _____
*   _____
*   _____
*   _____
*   _____
*   _____
*   _____
*   _____
*   _____
*   _____
*   _____
*   _____

Self-Authorized Team Leadership

Self-authorized team leadership is a form of "accountable follower-ship" in which team members assume responsibility for their performance and their relationships with other team members.

Self-authorized leadership is based on four assumptions:

- All team members practice some degree of self-authorized leadership.

- Self-authorized leadership is applicable to all team members.

- Not all team members are effective self-authorized leaders.

- Self-authorized leadership can be developed.

Notes

- _____
- _____
- _____
- _____
- _____
- _____
- _____
- _____
- _____
- _____
- _____
- _____
- _____
- _____
- _____
- _____
- _____
- _____
- _____
- _____
- _____

Self-Authorized Team Leadership (cont.)

To be successful, self-authorized leaders employ two types of strategies that serve to direct their development and performance:

- Behavioral strategies.

- Cognitive strategies.

Behavioral strategies

Behavioral strategies are self-directed action efforts that direct team member performance to excellence. The strategies are as follows:

BEHAVIORAL STRATEGIES

- Self-imposed outcomes.

- Self-management of workplace behaviors.

- Self-observations of outcomes.

- Self-rewards.

Notes

- _____

- _____

- _____

- _____

- _____

- _____

- _____

- _____

- _____

- _____

- _____

- _____

- _____

- _____

- _____

- _____

- _____

Self-Authorized Team Leadership (cont.)

Cognitive strategies

Cognitive strategies focus on the naturally rewarding aspects of teamwork. Four strategies that promote a positive attitude toward teamwork are as follows:

> ### COGNITIVE STRATEGIES
>
> - Self-knowledge.
> - Skill.
> - Self-control.
> - Purpose.

Notes

- _____
- _____
- _____
- _____
- _____
- _____
- _____
- _____
- _____
- _____
- _____
- _____
- _____
- _____
- _____
- _____
- _____
- _____

Increasing Leadership Effectiveness

Self-authorized team leaders who want to increase their effectiveness as team members can do so by using the following strategies:

INCREASING EFFECTIVENESS

- Maintaining an outcome orientation.
- Focusing attention.
- Leading others by example.
- Balancing the mind and heart.

Notes

- _____
- _____
- _____
- _____
- _____
- _____
- _____
- _____
- _____
- _____
- _____
- _____
- _____
- _____
- _____
- _____
- _____
- _____
- _____
- _____

Maintaining an Outcome Orientation

Maintaining an outcome orientation allows self-authorized team leaders to see their experiences as a set of choices. Rather than addressing the issue of "why" a problem exists, it organizes experience around "what" is wanted, and "how" it becomes possible to achieve it. When a specific outcome is decided upon, it becomes possible to turn those examples of not getting what you want into valuable feedback. You no longer fail at your endeavors but learn from your experiences.

Outcome exercise

Answer the following "outcome" questions. It is an individual exercise which means that you have to decide what it is you want. The "outcome" you decide upon should be initiated and maintained for you not someone else.

1. **What do you want? (Be specific.)**

   _____

   _____

2. **When do you want it?**

   _____

   _____

3. **How will you know that you have it?**

   _____

   _____

4. **When you get what you want, what else in your life will change?**

   _____

   _____

5. **What resources do you have available to help you get what you want today?**

   _____

   _____

6. **What is stopping you?**

   _____

   _____

Focusing Attention

Focusing attention refers to the ability to have a clear set of goals and priorities that result from maintaining an outcome orientation. People who are able to focus attention know where they are going and don't waste precious time getting there.

Leading Others by Example

Leading others by example is the "golden rule" of self-authorized team leadership. It refers to modeling appropriate behaviors such as respecting, supporting, listening, communicating, collaborating, and being sensitive to the needs of all team members.

Balancing the Mind and Heart

Balancing the mind and the heart allows self-authorized team leaders to engage both the subjective and analytical thinking processes of the mind. The goal is to create a balance, or alignment, between how we feel and think, which is necessary if we are going to be working effectively with other team members.

Notes

- _____
- _____
- _____
- _____
- _____
- _____
- _____
- _____
- _____
- _____
- _____
- _____
- _____
- _____
- _____
- _____
- _____
- _____

Leadership Character

An effective approach to empowering self-authorized team leaders is the adherence to the seven pillars of leadership character. The seven pillars are values that serve as a foundation for effective self-authorized team leadership.

SEVEN PILLARS OF LEADERSHIP CHARACTER

- Caring.
- Courage.
- Honesty.
- Integrity.
- Responsibility.
- Loyalty.
- Fairness.

Notes

- _____
- _____
- _____
- _____
- _____
- _____
- _____
- _____
- _____
- _____
- _____
- _____
- _____
- _____
- _____
- _____

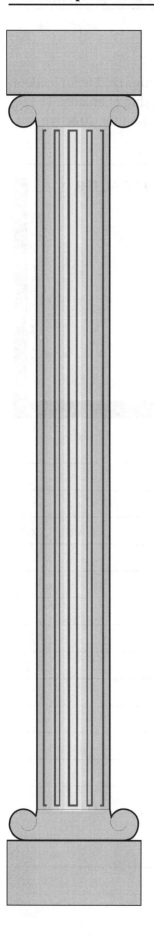

The Seven Pillars of Leadership Character

An effective approach to empowering self-authorized team leaders is the adherence to the seven pillars of leadership character. The seven pillars are values that serve as a foundation for effective self-authorized team leadership. The seven pillars that form the foundation are caring, courage, honesty, integrity, responsibility, loyalty, and fairness.

Caring

The ability to show others that you care about them through kindness, generosity, sharing, and compassion.

Courage

The attitude or response of facing and dealing with anything recognized as dangerous, difficult, or painful, instead of withdrawing from it.

Honesty

The willingness to be truthful and sincere without deceiving or misleading others or withholding important information in relationships of trust.

Integrity

The ability to stand up for your own beliefs about right and wrong and show commitment, courage, and self-discipline in everyday team member interactions.

Responsibility

The ability to think before you act, giving consideration to the possible consequences of your interactions as well as exercising self-control and self-discipline.

Loyalty

The willingness to stand by and support other team members without talking behind people's backs, spreading rumors, or engaging in harmful gossip.

Fairness

The ability to treat all team members alike without prejudgment and to make decisions only on appropriate considerations.

Self-authorized team leadership is a concept that places the responsibility of leadership on the shoulders of each team member. As team members assume responsibility for their actions and relationships with others, they share leadership responsibilities in all aspects of the team's work.

Chapter Eight:

Learning Activities

In this chapter, you will find activity guides for use during your training sessions. Each of the activity guides has one or both of the following components, depending on the nature of the activity and its use in the workshop.

- A set of instructions for your use during the activity. These instructions are in the same format as the training plans presented previously.

- Handouts to be reproduced and provided to participants during the activity.

USING THE PARTICIPANT HANDOUTS

You may use the participant pages in two ways:

- Key them into your word processing system "as is" or customize them to suit your specific needs.

- Photocopy the masters that you need from this book and use them "as is."

The following activities are not included in the training plans, but may be used to enhance your teambuilding training:

- *Team Purpose* (pp. 190-191)

- *What Team Stage Are We Going Through?* (pp. 191-194)

- *Team Interaction Activity (Sociogram)* (pp. 195-197)

- *Team Leadership: Finish the Sentence* (pp. 198-199)

- *Team Values* (pp. 200-201)

TRAINER'S NOTES

Team Purpose

Purpose   To help team members understand the purpose of the teams' existence.

Timing   20 minutes.

GROUP ACTIVITY

 PRESENT the following instructions to the group:

Individually, write your responses to the three questions on the *Team Purpose Worksheet*.

 ASK this question:

• Are there any questions about what you will be doing?

Answer the questions, as appropriate.

 ASK participants to start filling out their worksheets.

When everyone has finished, *POST* different team purpose responses on a flip chart.

Process the information presented by the participants and look for similarities.

GROUP DISCUSSION

ASK the participants if they see any similarity in the responses, and process the learnings from the experience.

ASK these questions:

• What was there about the exercise that was helpful to you as a participant?

• Do you better understand the perceptions that are shared by other participants?

Look for answers such as those that allow you to lead the group to a conclusion about the exercise:

• The team has a clear awareness concerning the team's purpose.

• Team members can see the similarities and differences of other team members.

HANDOUT   **Team Purpose Worksheet**

Instructions   Complete the following statements individually and discuss.

1. **The purpose for this team's existence is:**

   _____

   _____

   _____

   _____

   _____

   _____

   _____

   _____

   _____

2. **Our task as a team is to:**

   _____

   _____

   _____

   _____

   _____

   _____

   _____

   _____

3. **We will be successful as a team if we do:**

   _____

   _____

   _____

   _____

   _____

   _____

   _____

   _____

TRAINER'S NOTES

What Team Stage Are We Going Through?

Purpose   To understand the stages of team development and where the team is at any given point in time.

Timing   15 minutes.

GROUP ACTIVITY

PRESENT the following instructions:

1. On the worksheet provided, read the situation and determine the stage of team development.

2. Be prepared to discuss your responses.

ASK this question:

• Are there any questions about what you will be doing?

Answer the questions, as appropriate.

ASK participants to start filling out their worksheets.

After everyone has finished, *POST* the responses Team Stages on a flipchart.

Keep track of the correct responses and keep charting until all responses are given.

Answer key   Question 1: Performing

Question 2: Norming

Question 3: Forming

Question 4: Storming

GROUP DISCUSSION

ASK the team if there are any questions concerning the stages and process the learnings from the discussion.

GROUP ACTIVITY

SAY:

In small groups, discuss your responses.

Reconvene the large group and *ASK*:

- What was there about this exercise that you found particularly insightful?

Look for answers that allow you to lead the group to a conclusion such as this about the exercise.

- All groups go through stages of development.
- There is a sequence of stages.
- All stages must be experienced.

<u>HANDOUT</u>

Instructions

Team Stages Worksheet

Determine the stage of team development by the information that is provided below. Select from the following responses:

Forming   Storming   Norming   Performing

1. **What stage incorporates the following?**

   a. A new ability to express criticism constructively.

   b. Acceptance of membership in the team.

   c. Relief that it seems like everything will work out.

   Response: _____

2. **What stage incorporates the following?**

   a. Members have insight into personal and group processes, and better understanding of each other's strength and weaknesses.

   b. Satisfaction of the team's progress.

   Response: _____

3. **What stage incorporates the following?**

   a. Excitement, anticipation, and optimism.

   b. Initial, tentative attachment to the team.

   c. Anxiety about the job ahead.

   Response: _____

4. **What stage incorporates the following?**

   a. Resistance to the task.

   b. Sharp fluctuations in attitude.

   Response: _____

TRAINER'S NOTES   Team Interaction Activity (Sociogram)

Purpose

To draw a team sociogram. The sociogram can help the team understand the interaction patterns of team members.

Timing

15 minutes.

GROUP ACTIVITY

PRESENT the following instructions:

1. You will be working in small groups.

2. On the worksheet provided, put the names of the members of your team in their seating arrangement.

3. When someone speaks, indicate that they have spoken by putting a mark by the individual's name.

4. When a person speaks, draw an arrow from the person who speaks to the person that responds.

ASK this question:

- Are there any questions about what you will be doing?

Answer the questions, as appropriate.

ASK participants to break into small groups and start filling out their worksheets.

After everyone has finished, *POST* the responses on a Team Interaction flipchart.

Keep track of the responses.

Keep charting until all responses are given.

GROUP DISCUSSION

ASK the team if there are any questions concerning the team sociogram, and process the learnings from the discussion.

GROUP ACTIVITY

 PRESENT the following instructions:

In small groups, discuss your sociograms.

 Reconvene the large group and *ASK* this question:

• What was there about this exercise that you found particularly insightful?

Look for answers such as these that allow you to lead the group to a conclusion about the exercise:

• Who spoke the most in the group?

• Did all team members have a chance to talk?

• Was anyone left out?

HANDOUT   Team Interaction Worksheet

Instructions   Place the names of all team members in their appropriate positions in the space below. Indicate by putting a mark by the person's name when they speak. Draw an arrow from the person that speaks to the person who responds. Use the example below as a guide.

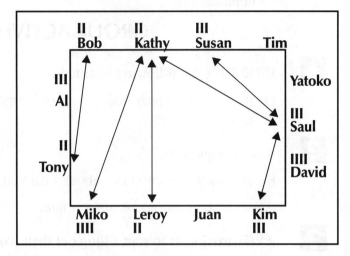

Team Leadership: Finish the Sentence

Purpose   To determine the characteristics of a good team leader. By the end of the activity, each team member will have an opportunity to discuss team leadership characteristics.

Timing   15 minutes.

GROUP ACTIVITY

PRESENT the following instructions:

On the worksheet provided, place your responses in the appropriate areas.

ASK this question:

• Are there any questions about what you will be doing?

Answer the questions, as appropriate.

ASK participants to start filling out their worksheets.

After everyone has finished, post the Team Leadership responses on a flipchart.

Keep track of the responses.

Keep charting until all responses are given.

GROUP DISCUSSION

ASK the team if there are any questions concerning team member responses.

Process the learnings from the discussion.

GROUP ACTIVITY

SAY:

In small groups, discuss your responses.

Reconvene the large group and *ASK* this question:

• What was there about this exercise that you found particularly insightful?

Look for answers such as these that allow you to lead the group to a conclusion about the exercise:

• Were the characteristics similar?

• Leadership is an important part of team dynamics.

• All team members are leaders.

HANDOUT   **Team Leadership Worksheet**

Instructions   Answer the following questions as quickly as possible.

1. **A good leader always . . .**

_____

_____

_____

_____

_____

2. **The role of the leader of the team is to . . .**

_____

_____

_____

_____

_____

3. **A leader is one who . . .**

_____

_____

_____

_____

_____

4. **Some leaders are ineffective because they . . .**

_____

_____

_____

_____

TRAINER'S NOTES

Team Values

Purpose
To offer team members the opportunity to examine their values as they relate to team membership.

Timing
20 minutes.

GROUP ACTIVITY

PRESENT the following instructions:

On the worksheet provided, place your responses in the appropriate areas.

ASK this question:

• Are there any questions about what you will be doing?

Answer the questions, as appropriate.

ASK participants to start filling out their worksheets.

After everyone has finished, post the Team Values responses on a flipchart.

Keep track of the responses.

Keep charting until all responses are given.

GROUP DISCUSSION

ASK the team if there are any questions concerning team member responses.

PROCESS the learnings from the discussion.

GROUP ACTIVITY

SAY:.

In small groups, discuss your responses.

Reconvene the large group and *ASK* this question:

• What was there about this exercise that you found particularly insightful?

Look for answers such as these that will allow you to lead the group to a conclusion about the exercise:

• Values are similar throughout the team.

• Values form the foundation for effective teams.

• Values are motivational forces that influence what we do.

HANDOUT

Team Values Worksheet

Instructions

Answer the following questions and list the things that are important to you as a team member. Be prepared to discuss your responses.

1. **The five most important things about work are . . .**

_____

_____

_____

_____

_____

_____

_____

2. **The five most important things about being a good team member are . . .**

_____

_____

_____

_____

_____

_____

_____

3. **The five most important things about being a good friend are . . .**

_____

_____

_____

_____

_____

_____

_____

Feedback Activity

Purpose

To give team members experience in giving and receiving feedback in a constructive manner. This will allow them to strengthen their communication processes and grow as a team.

Tming

15 minutes.

BENEFITS OF GIVING FEEDBACK

- Feedback reduces uncertainty.

- Feedback solves problems.

- Feedback builds trust.

- Feedback can strengthen relationships.

- Feedback improves work quality.

PRESENT the following instructions:

Using the worksheets provided, choose an example of Giving and Receiving Feedback and illustrate the characteristic you have chosen.

ASK this question:

- Are there any questions about what you will be doing?

Answer the questions, as appropriate.

ASK participants to start filling out their worksheets.

After everyone has finished, post the responses on a flipchart.

Keep track of the responses.

Keep charting until all responses are given.

<u>**HANDOUT**</u>   **Giving Feedback**

1. Consider how your team members practice giving feedback. Which description below characterizes how your team gives feedback to each other?

   a. **Expressed directly.**

      Feedback is specific, clearly describing observable behavior and specific incidents.

   b. **Descriptive.**

      Feedback is nonjudgmental, making no evaluation of the other person's intentions.

   c. **Timely.**

      Feedback is given close to the time of the incident or observation, containing no accumulation of grievances.

   d. **On-going.**

      Feedback is not a one-time event, but a process of offering useful information for continuous improvement.

2. Give an example that illustrates the characteristic you have chosen.

   _____

   _____

   _____

   _____

   _____

   _____

   _____

   _____

   _____

   _____

   _____

   _____

   _____

   _____

   _____

   _____

<u>**HANDOUT**</u>   **Receiving Feedback**

1. Consider how your team members practice receiving feedback. Which description below characterizes how your team receives feedback from each other?

   a. **Solicits feedback.**

   Recipient encourages specific feedback, using clear and concrete questions to probe the giver.

   b. **Doesn't get defensive.**

   Recipient listens without interrupting, explaining, or defending his behavior. Avoids the word "but" which refutes and denies the feedback offered.

   c. **Uses the feedback.**

   Feedback is welcomed by recipient, examined for usefulness, and used to make changes in behavior.

2. Give an example that illustrates the characteristic you have chosen.

   _____

   _____

   _____

   _____

   _____

   _____

   _____

   _____

   _____

   _____

   _____

   _____

   _____

   _____

Chapter Nine:

Tools and Assessments

In this chapter, you will find assessments for use during your team-building training sessions. As with the learning activities in the previous chapter, each of the assessments will have these components.

• A set of instructions for your use during the assessment. These instructions are in the same format as the training plans presented previously.

• A participant page that needs to be reproduced and provided to participants for the assessment.

USING THE TOOLS AND ASSESSMENTS

You may use the tools and assessments in two ways :

• Key them into your word processing system "as is" or customize them to suit your specific needs.

• Photocopy the masters that you need from this book and use them "as is."

The following tools and assessments are not included in the training plans, but may be used to enhance your teambuilding training:

• *Organizational Team Readiness Survey (OTRS)* (pp. 206-214)

• *Team Style Survey (TSS)* (pp. 221-227)

TRAINER'S NOTES

Organizational Team Readiness Survey (OTRS)

Purpose

The OTRS is designed to determine the extent to which an organization's management philosophy and core values, structure, problem-solving, groups, information systems, physical and technical design, reward systems, personnel policies, career systems, selection systems, training orientation, and leadership style are in alignment to create and support a work team environment.

Timing

20 minutes.

GROUP ACTIVITY

PRESENT the following instructions:

1. Read the following OTRS sections before you begin the survey.

   • *Administering the OTRS.*

   • *Scoring and Interpreting the OTRS.*

   • *Definition of Terms.*

2. Mark your answers to the questions.

3. After completing the OTRS, turn to the Scoring Grid and score your results.

4. Then, read the interpretation of your scores.

ASK this question:

• Are there any questions about what you will be doing?

Answer the questions appropriately.

ASK participants to start answering the questions.

GROUP DISCUSSION

PROCESS the responses using a flipchart.

Ask these questions:

• What did you learn about your organization's readiness for establishing a work team system?

• What are the areas that you can work toward developing?

Validity of the OTRS

The *Organizational Team Readiness Survey* (OTRS) is designed to assess an organization's readiness to establish a work team system. The OTRS determines the extent to which an organization's management philosophy and core values, structure, problem-solving groups, information systems, physical and technical design, reward systems, personnel policies, career systems, selection systems, training orientation, and leadership style are in alignment to create and support a work team environment.

The *Organizational Team Readiness Survey's* (OTRS) *Definition of Terms* section was evaluated by five organizational development specialists for accuracy in term definition. There was 100% agreement on all eleven variables used in the OTRS.

The OTRS was administered to thirty-two mid-level managers attending a Human Interaction Laboratory conducted by the National Training Lab Institute for Applied Behavioral Sciences. The respondents were asked to respond by either agreeing or disagreeing with the following questions concerning the OTRS:

- Is the survey easy to read?
  (75% agreement)

- Did you understand the *Definition of Terms* section?
  (100% agreement)

- Were the definitions in the *Definition of Terms* section applicable to your organization?
  (100% agreement)

- Did your final score on the OTRS assist you in understanding the readiness level of your organization to use teams?
  (100% agreement).

Administering the OTRS

The OTRS can be used as a data collection instrument or in team-building activities. When administering the OTRS, allow 20 minutes to complete.

Scoring and Interpreting the OTRS

The OTRS is self-scoring which allows respondents to score each variable independent of other variables. After completing the survey, ensure that the participants accurately compute their scores for each organizational variable in the survey. Transfer scores from each question to the answer grid at the end of the survey. This will allow respondents to visually see their scores in relation to all the variables measured.

Total all scores for each of the eleven variables. Place scores in the scoring grid. Attach the following point value to each selection.

> **Never = 1**
>
> **Seldom = 2**
>
> **Occasionally = 3**
>
> **Often = 4**
>
> **Always = 5**

Score 5 - 12   Considered low and suggests that the corresponding system will not support the establishment of a work team environment.

Score 13 - 17   Considered moderate and suggests that the corresponding system may support the establishment of a work team environment. There is some potential with this type of score but the system must constantly be reevaluated to ensure support for implementing a work team system.

Score 18 - 25   Considered High and suggests that the corresponding system will support the establishment of a work team environment. This range of score suggests that the organization can consider implementing a work teams.

Any organization that has moderate to high scores in a greater percentage of the eleven variables will be able to initiate action to establish work teams with success.

If a greater number of the variable scores fall in the low range, the organization may have difficulty institutionalizing a work team system and environment.

<u>HANDOUT</u>   ## Definition of Terms

Management Philosophy and Core Values

The organization's guiding principles that articulate assumptions about people and how the business is run.

Organization Structure

The levels of management and functions of staff support where decision making is centered.

Problem-Solving Groups

Task forces, quality circles, and other activities addressed by employee participation practices.

Information Systems

The method of information sharing and exchange which provides employees with the means to coordinate and manage work systems.

Physical and Technical Work Design

The extent to which the work environment is safe, pleasant, centralized, and employee stratified.

Reward Systems

The extent to which the organization calls for skill-based pay, gainsharing, profit sharing, employee ownership, flexible benefits, an all-salary workforce, with an open, participative decision-making process.

Personnel Policies

Issues related to hours of work, flex-time, types of benefits offered, layoff, discipline, and other issues that are typically decided by management.

Career Systems

The career options available in an organization with adequate counseling to support information systems.

Selection Systems

The manner in which applicants are assessed for their skills and attitudes toward work in the organization.

Training Orientation

The level and commitment the organization has towards developing its employee body.

Leadership Style

The methods management uses to inspire loyalty, commitment, and motivation in the workforce

<u>HANDOUT</u>   **Organizational Team Readiness Survey (OTRS)**

Instructions   1. You have 20 minutes to complete the OTRS.

2. Select from five responses.

3. Then, tally your responses according to the values listed below.

Never = 1   Seldom = 2   Occasionally = 3   Often = 4   Always = 5

OTRS Instrument	Never				Always
1. My organization treats its employees with respect.	1	2	3	4	5
2. My organization considers employees valuable assets.	1	2	3	4	5
3. My organization supports employee decision-making at the lowest level.	1	2	3	4	5
4. My organization supports information sharing among all employees.	1	2	3	4	5
5. My organization has a commitment to developing all its employees.	1	2	3	4	5

Management Philosophy and Core Values Score: Total _____

6. My organization's management structure has few levels.	1	2	3	4	5
7. My organization has a structure where some staff activities are accomplished by line employees.	1	2	3	4	5
8. My organization's management staff functions more as coaches and consultants to employees.	1	2	3	4	5
9. My organization has a decentralized management structure.	1	2	3	4	5
10. My organization gives responsibility to work units for maintaining a product, service, or customer.	1	2	3	4	5

Organization Structure Score: Total _____

11. My organization uses quality improvement groups.	1	2	3	4	5
12. My organization uses task forces to deal with important job related issues.	1	2	3	4	5
13. My organization has training programs which teach employee problem-solving and team skills.	1	2	3	4	5
14. My organization has a suggestion program.	1	2	3	4	5
15. My organization supports the idea that work related issues are best resolved by employees closest to the problem.	1	2	3	4	5

Problem-Solving Group Score: Total _____

		Never				Always
16.	My organization has an information system which provides feedback about company issues to all levels in the company.	1	2	3	4	5
17.	My organization encourages feedback from all employees.	1	2	3	4	5
18.	My organization allows direct communication between employees for the purpose of coordinating their work activities.	1	2	3	4	5
19.	My organization has a decentralized information system.	1	2	3	4	5
20.	My organization ensures that all employees understand how the business is doing.	1	2	3	4	5

Information Systems Score: **Total** _____

		Never				Always
21.	My organization supports a participative work environment.	1	2	3	4	5
22.	My organization does not use status symbols such as reserved parking spaces, executive washrooms, or dining rooms	1	2	3	4	5
23.	My organization has a dress code that emphasizes company identity rather than status differences.	1	2	3	4	5
24.	My organization has designed a physical layout which creates an open working atmosphere.	1	2	3	4	5
25.	My organization is made up of small work units which are easily identified.	1	2	3	4	5

Physical and Technical Design Score: **Total** _____

		Never				Always
26.	My organization has a pay system based on skill proficiency.	1	2	3	4	5
27.	My organization pays a bonus to employees based on improvements in the operating results of the company	1	2	3	4	5
28.	My organization has a flexible benefits plan.	1	2	3	4	5
29.	My organization has an all salaried work force.	1	2	3	4	5
30.	My organization has an open information system in regards to salary decisions.	1	2	3	4	5

Reward Systems Score: **Total** _____

OTRS Instrument   **Never**   **Always**

31. My organization's personnel policies reflect the needs of the work force.	1 2 3 4 5
32. My organization's personnel policies allow individuals a choice and recognize diversity among the work force.	1 2 3 4 5
33. My organization attempts to avoid layoffs.	1 2 3 4 5
34. My organization supports employees in areas such as flex-time, types of benefits offered, and discipline.	1 2 3 4 5
35. My organization would rather have a work week reduction than down size the work force.	1 2 3 4 5

Personnel Policies Score: **Total** _____

36. My organization supports skill-based training.	1 2 3 4 5
37. My organization provides employees counseling concerning the skills that are need to perform the work..	1 2 3 4 5
38. My organization recognizes that employees have different career orientations and attempts to find a career direction that fits their preference.	1 2 3 4 5
39. My organization provides skill-based pay for managers as well as line employees.	1 2 3 4 5
40. My organization announces career opportunities within the organization.	1 2 3 4 5

Career Systems Score: **Total** _____

41. My organization hires employees who have an orientation towards learning and developing.	1 2 3 4 5
42. My organization hires and promotes employees who are willing to be responsible for their own behavior.	1 2 3 4 5
43. My organization considers good interpersonal skills and the willingness to work in groups an important criteria for advancement.	1 2 3 4 5
44. My organization gives prospective employees a realistic job preview.	1 2 3 4 5
45. My organization encourages employees to be involved in the selection and hiring process.	1 2 3 4 5

Selection System Score: **Total** _____

OTRS Instrument   Never   Always

46. My organization has a high level commitment and capability for training the work force.   1   2   3   4   5

47. My organization encourages employees to continue developing their job and interpersonal skills.   1   2   3   4   5

48. My organization supports technical training.   1   2   3   4   5

49. My organization supports training in problem-solving, decision-making, and group skills development.   1   2   3   4   5

50. My organization shares with the employee body its economic situation as part of training.   1   2   3   4   5

Training Orientation Score: **Total** _____

51. My organization supports leader/managers who energize and motivate employees.   1   2   3   4   5

52. My organization's leadership provides a sense of direction and purpose.   1   2   3   4   5

53. My organization's key positions are staffed by people-oriented leaders.   1   2   3   4   5

54. My organization's leadership takes responsibility for the organization's culture and long-term goals.   1   2   3   4   5

55. My organization's leadership "walks their talk."   1   2   3   4   5

Leadership Style Score: **Total** _____

End of OTRS
Move to Scoring Grid

HANDOUT

OTRS Scoring Grid

After completing the survey, total each of the eleven category scores and transfer the cumulative total to the scoring grid below.

The greater the number of variables that are in the Moderate to High range, the greater chances are that your organization will support a work team environment.

Five key indicators that must be in the Moderate to High range are Philosophy and Values, Organization Structure, Personnel Policies, Training Orientation, and Leadership Style. If these indicators fall in the Low range, the organization will have a difficult time developing a team environment.

If a greater number of category scores fall in the Low range, the organization is not ready to move to a team environment. Work can be accomplished in each category to move toward an organizational philosophy that supports the team concept.

OTRS Scoring Grid

Category	5 - 12 Low	13 - 17 Moderate	18 - 25 High
Philosophy and Values			
Organization Structure			
Problem-Solving			
Information Systems			
P & T Design			
Reward Systems			
Personnel Policies			
Career Systems			
Selection System			
Training Orientation			
Leadership Style			

TRAINER'S NOTES

Team Building Instrument (TBI)

Purpose

The *Team Building Instrument* (TBI) is designed to examine individual perceptions of team strengths and weaknesses in six areas related to team development. The six areas are: team purpose, stages of team development, team member roles, team communication, team processes, and team leadership. The results identify specific areas where teambuilding efforts can be focused.

Timing

10 minutes.

GROUP ACTIVITY

PRESENT the following instructions.

1. Read the following TBI sections before you begin the survey.

   • *Administering the TBI.*

   • *Interpreting the TBI.*

2. Mark you answers to the questions.

3. Upon completion of the TBI, turn to the *Scoring Grid* to interpret your scores.

ASK this question:

• Are there any questions about what you will be doing?

Answer the questions appropriately.

ASK participants to start answering the questions.

GROUP DISCUSSION

PROCESS the responses using a flipchart.

ASK these questions:

• What did you learn about your team's strengths and weaknesses?

• Where can you focus your teambuilding efforts?

LOOK for answers to guide the group to a specific outcome.

Administering the TBI

The Team Building Instrument (TBI) is designed to examine individual perceptions of team strengths and weaknesses in six areas related to team development. The six areas are as follows: team purpose, stages of team development, team member roles, team communication, team processes, and team leadership. The results identify specific areas where teambuilding efforts can be focused.

The TBI can be used for collecting relevant data for designing teambuilding training interventions or it can be used as a stand-alone teambuilding activity. Allow 10 minutes to completed.

Interpreting the TBI

Category	Questions
1. Team Purpose	1-5
2. Stages of Team Development	6-10
3. Team Member Roles	11-15
4. Team Communication	16-20
5. Team Processes	21-25
6. Team Leadership	26-30

Examine each of the six areas to determine whether or not there is agreement or disagreement in the response categories. The greater number of Agree responses in each category, the less time is needed to focus on the component during teambuilding events. Similarly, the greater number of Disagree responses in each category, the more time is needed to focus on the area during teambuilding training.

Example #1

In example #1, the respondent perceives that Team Communication (Agree = 1) (Disagree = 4) and Team Leadership (Agree = 0 and Disagree = 5) are areas where the team needs development. Discuss reasons why the team is not successful in these categories.

Example #1	Agree	Disagree
Team Purpose	4	1
Stages of Team Development	4	1
Team Member Roles	5	0
Team Communication	1	4
Team Processes	3	2
Team Leadership	0	5

Example #2

In example #2, the respondent perceives the team doing well in all six categories. Discuss reason for team success in each category.

Example #2	Agree	Disagree
Team Purpose	5	0
Stages of Team Development	5	0
Team Member Roles	5	0
Team Communication	5	0
Team Processes	5	0
Team Leadership	5	0

<u>HANDOUT</u>   **Team Building Instrument (TBI)**

Instructions   1. Answer the questions as you see your team functioning.

2. You have 10 minutes to complete the TBI.

3. Check either Agree or Disagree as your response choices.

4. Place the number of Agree or Disagree responses in the grid at the end of the instrument.

TBI	**Agree**	**Disagree**

I. Team Purpose

1. My team is driven by a clear desired future state. _____ _____

2. My team fully understands its mission. _____ _____

3. My team is aware of the principles that govern how the team operates. _____ _____

4. My team has clearly defined goals that it strives to achieve. _____ _____

5. My team is energized and motivated to succeed. _____ _____

Total Ratings: _____ _____

II. Stages of Team Development

6. Team members are aware of the stages of team development. _____ _____

7. Team members understand the interpersonal issues that operate in the team. _____ _____

8. Team members understand group behavioral patterns. _____ _____

9. Team members can manage conflict in a supportive way. _____ _____

10. Team members can manage team issues collaboratively. _____ _____

Total Ratings: _____ _____

III Team Member Roles

11. Team members understand "task" and "process" roles. _____ _____

12. Team members understand the roles that can either facilitate or hinder team interaction. _____ _____

13. Team members can identify negative process behaviors. _____ _____

14. Team members know how to handle negative process behaviors. _____ _____

15. Team members can identify positive process roles. _____ _____

Total Ratings: _____ _____

TBI	Agree	Disagree

IV. Team Communication

16.　Team members share information effectively.　＿＿＿＿＿　＿＿＿＿＿

17.　Team members can give constructive feedback.　＿＿＿＿＿　＿＿＿＿＿

18.　Team members listen well to each other.　＿＿＿＿＿　＿＿＿＿＿

19.　Team members work through barriers that can block effective communication.　＿＿＿＿＿　＿＿＿＿＿

20.　Team members share a common language.　＿＿＿＿＿　＿＿＿＿＿

　　Total Ratings:　＿＿＿＿＿　＿＿＿＿＿

V.　Team Processes

21.　My team manages conflict effectively.　＿＿＿＿＿　＿＿＿＿＿

22.　My team has a decision-making process that works.　＿＿＿＿＿　＿＿＿＿＿

23.　My team uses a step-by-step problem-solving process.　＿＿＿＿＿　＿＿＿＿＿

24.　My team plans meetings that encourage participation.　＿＿＿＿＿　＿＿＿＿＿

25.　My team effectively manages the diversity of the team.　＿＿＿＿＿　＿＿＿＿＿

　　Total Ratings:　＿＿＿＿＿　＿＿＿＿＿

VI. Team Leadership

26.　The team leader manages the team effectively.　＿＿＿＿＿　＿＿＿＿＿

27.　The team leader creates opportunities for the team.　＿＿＿＿＿　＿＿＿＿＿

28.　The team leader knows how to get things done.　＿＿＿＿＿　＿＿＿＿＿

29.　The team leader encourages active participation.　＿＿＿＿＿　＿＿＿＿＿

30.　The team leader guides and facilitates the team effort.　＿＿＿＿＿　＿＿＿＿＿

　　Total Ratings:　＿＿＿＿＿　＿＿＿＿＿

End of TBI

Move to Scoring Grid

TBI Scoring Grid

Refer back to each category in the TBI and place the numbers of Agree or Disagree in the corresponding categories below.

Interpreting the TBI

Category	Agree	Disagree
Team Purpose		
Stages of Team Development		
Team Member Roles		
Team Communication		
Team Processes		
Team Leadership		

Some things to consider about your ratings:

- **Is there any one category that has a high or low rating?**

  If this is the case, you may want to examine the category more closely to determine the reasons for the scores.

- **Do several categories have a Disagree high rating?**

  If this is the case, consider how your team may not be getting the job done. Discuss the reasons for your perceptions. This is an opportunity to gain clarity on what the team needs to work on to be successful.

TRAINER'S NOTES	# Team Style Survey (TSS)

Purpose

The *Team Style Survey* (TSS) is designed to reveal the most appropriate team style for an organization based on three athletic team models: baseball, football, and basketball. The TSS assesses the following key team indicators: roles, tasks, skills, control, and work design. The relationships of the above indicators to the organization's work will determine the type of team best suited to accomplish the organization's overall mission.

Timing

10 minutes.

GROUP ACTIVITY

PRESENT the following instructions.

1. Read the following TSS sections before you begin the survey.

   • *Administering the Team Style Survey (TSS).*

   • *Scoring and Interpreting the TSS.*

2. Mark you answers to the questions.

3. Upon completion of the TSS, turn to the TSS Scoring Grid and score your results.

4. Read the interpretation of your scores.

ASK this question:

• Are there any questions about what you will be doing?

Answer the questions appropriately.

ASK participants to start answering the questions.

GROUP DISCUSSION

PROCESS the responses using a flipchart.

ASK these questions:

• What team style is best suited for your organization?

• Is the team style best for accomplishing both the work and the mission of the organization?

Look for answers that indicate that the team models are understood.

Validity of the TSS

The *Team Style Survey* (TSS) is designed to reveal the most appropriate team style for an organization based on three athletic team models: baseball, football, and basketball. The TSS assesses the following key team indicators: roles, tasks, skills, control, and work design.

The *Team Style Survey* (TSS) was administered to thirty-two mid-level managers attending a Human Interaction Laboratory conducted by the National Training Lab Institute For Applied Behavioral Sciences. The respondents were asked to respond by either agreeing or disagreeing to the following questions:

- When you read the survey, is it easy to read and understand? (100% agreement)

- Does the team analogy fit your organization? (90% agreement)

- Did the results of the TSS help you to identify your organization's most appropriate team style? (100% agreement).

Administering the Team Style Survey (TSS)

The *Team Style Survey* (TSS) can be used in teambuilding sessions or any educational activity designed for gaining a greater understanding of team models that can be used in the workplace. When administering the survey, give participants 10 to 15 minutes to complete the task.

Ask participants to answer the questions based on their understanding of how people work together and how they see the work being accomplished in the organization. Use the following responses to the questions.

Seldom = 1

Sometimes = 2

Always = 3

Scoring and Interpreting the TSS

The *Team Style Survey* (TSS) is a self-scoring instrument. After completing the survey, ensure that the participants accurately total their responses. Score value for each response will be either a 1, 2, or 3. Ask participants to transfer their response scores to the scoring grid at the end of the survey. The highest cumulative score identifies the team model that an organization can use to accomplish its work.

Discuss the team analogy and relate it to work designs in organizations. This discussion can last from 15 to 30 minutes depending on the size and questions asked by participants. There will be variations of team models that can be discussed.

HANDOUT	**Team Style Survey**

Instructions

1. You have 10 minutes to complete the TSS.

2. Select from three responses: Seldom, Sometimes, Always.

3. After completing the survey, place the corresponding point value of your answers into the appropriate response category on the Scoring Grid. The highest cumulative score in the grid reflects the team design that is most appropriate for your organization.

Scoring

Seldom = 1 point

Sometimes = 2 points

Always = 3 points

The TSS	Seldom	Sometimes	Always
1. Each team member works relatively independent of other team members.	1	2	3
2. Execution of team tasks is coordinated through a comprehensive prerehearsed plan of action.	1	2	3
3. Team members must be flexible and able to assume one another's work responsibilities at any time.	1	2	3
4. Team members are expected to exercise their knowledge and influence in their areas of expertise.	1	2	3
5. Team success can only be achieved if all team member actions are carefully coordinated.	1	2	3
6. Team members must work together smoothly complementing each other's actions.	1	2	3
7. Team members must be able to carry out a variety of independent tasks, the order and priorities of which can change unpredictably.	1	2	3
8. Team tasks must be carried out in a predetermined sequence of actions and in a controlled manner.	1	2	3
9. All team members participate actively and take the initiative when they feel it is necessary.	1	2	3
10. All tasks by team members contribute to the end product.	1	2	3
11. All team members contribute to the tasks and each must pull their own weight.	1	2	3
12. Team members interact constantly in a wide variety of ways and can rapidly adapt to changing circumstance.	1	2	3
13. Team members do not work in close collaboration with each other. Any interactions between team members is brief and infrequent.	1	2	3

TSS	Seldom	Sometimes	Always
14. Team members must interact frequently and must tailor their communication styles to suit the task at hand.	1	2	3
15. Team members frequently swap jobs and positions as circumstances change.	1	2	3
16. Team members are often widely dispersed geographically.	1	2	3
17. All team members are involved in every aspect of the work that the team accomplishes.	1	2	3
18. Team member activity is often viewed as frenetic movement that culminates in task accomplishment.	1	2	3
19. Team interaction occurs only between a few team members who work closely together during any activity.	1	2	3
20. Team member coordination is achieved through planning and hierarchical direction.	1	2	3
21. Team members must be able to function as a unit without precise direction.	1	2	3

End of the TSS

Move to Scoring Grid

HANDOUT   **TSS Scoring Grid**

Instructions   1. To determine the team style best suited for accomplishing the work in your organization, complete the scoring below as directed.

2. Place the corresponding number response from the survey questions in the appropriate category below. Each response number identifies a particular team style. The highest cumulative score of all the categories represents the team design that your organization may wish to use to accomplish the work.

TSS Scoring Grid

1. _____	2. _____	3. _____
4. _____	5. _____	6. _____
7. _____	8. _____	9. _____
10. _____	11. _____	12. _____
13. _____	14. _____	15. _____
16. _____	17. _____	18. _____
19. _____	20. _____	21. _____
Total _____	Total _____	Total _____
Baseball Team Style	**Football Team Style**	**Basketball Team Style**

<u>**HANDOUT**</u>   **Sports Synopsis**

Baseball

Baseball is a highly individualistic sport that occasionally requires teamwork in certain circumstances. Players interact minimally, and coordination of players is achieved through the design of the game.

Football

Football demands organized, systematic teamwork. Plays are designed in advance, and players are assigned specialized roles throughout the game and for each play. Careful planning ensures player cooperation and collaboration.

Basketball

Basketball players are required to achieve spontaneous teamwork. Coordination is achieved as the players mutually and sometimes simultaneously adjust to the changing circumstances of the game. Basketball is a fast moving game requiring great flexibility and harmony among its players.

Leadership Role Checklist

Purpose

To focus team attention on how they deal with self leadership, to identify areas that need improvement as well as those areas that are sound, and to focus on individual leadership roles and how they affect the team.

Timing

10 minutes.

GROUP ACTIVITY

PRESENT the following instructions:

1. Fill out the Leadership Checklist.

2. Mark your first answer to each question.

3. After everyone has finished their individual checklists, ask for a show of hands for each question and total the responses on a flip chart.

ASK this question:

• Are there any questions about what you will be doing?

Answer the questions, as appropriate.

ASK participants to start filling out their checklists.

GROUP DISCUSSION

PROCESS the responses, using the flipchart.

ASK this question:

• What was there about this exercise that you found particularly insightful?

Look for answers to guide the group to a conclusion such as this about the exercise:

• The exercise was somewhat artificial.

• Nonetheless, under the best circumstances, it is difficult to be a good leader.

<u>**HANDOUT**</u>   **Leadership Role Checklist**

Yes	No	**Descriptions**
_____	_____	**1.** Are contributions to teamwork shared?
_____	_____	**2.** Are team decisions equally shared?
_____	_____	**3.** Is the role of meeting facilitator routinely rotated through natural rotation?
_____	_____	**4.** Does the team monitor its own objectives?
_____	_____	**5.** Is the role of leader shared when working on projects?
_____	_____	**6.** Is the role of team watchdog (monitor of team procedures and processes) shared?
_____	_____	**7.** Is the role of team representative, or liaison with other groups, shared?
_____	_____	**8.** Do the team members support each other when seeking conflict resolution?
_____	_____	**9.** Does everyone on the team bring information to the team?
_____	_____	**10.** Do team members encourage each other to contribute?

Team Development Rating Form

Purpose   To let the team understand and monitor their development through the different stages they encounter. With an understanding of where the team is, the stages can be passed through more effectively, resulting in greater cohesion.

Timing   15 minutes.

GROUP ACTIVITY

PRESENT the following instructions:

1. Fill out the *Team Development Rating Form*.

2. Mark your first answer to each question.

3. Total the number of responses to each question for your group.

ASK this question:

- Are there any questions about what you will be doing?

Answer the questions, as appropriate.

ASK participants to start filling out their forms.

After everyone has finished their individual forms, ask for a show of hands and mark the totals for each group on a flipchart.

Count the number of responses to each question.

For example: There were two people who responded to question #1 with a rating of 5 (strongly agree), there were three people who responded with a rating of 3 (undecided).

Keep charting until the responses to all questions have been tallied.

GROUP DISCUSSION

ASK the team if there are any surprises that show up on a flipchart.

Process the learnings from the different totals. What does it mean if everyone strongly agreed? What does it mean if no one agreed?

ASK this question:

- What was there about this exercise that you found particularly insightful?

Look for answers that allow you to lead the group to a conclusion such as this about the exercise.

- The exercise did not apply to where we are as a team.

- The exercise allows us to move more readily to the next stage.

<u>HANDOUT</u>   Team Development Rating Form

Strongly Disagree	Disagree	Undecided	Agree	Strongly Agree	Descriptions
1	2	3	4	5	**1.** The team's purpose is clear and understandable .
1	2	3	4	5	**2.** Everyone is included in all aspects of team business .
1	2	3	4	5	**3.** There is a comfortableness to being in team meetings .
1	2	3	4	5	**4.** Team discussions are open and free spirited .
1	2	3	4	5	**5.** The team utilizes everyone's abilities to the fullest possible extent .
1	2	3	4	5	**6.** There is encouragement and support for team members .
1	2	3	4	5	**7.** The team deals with conflict in an open, supportive way .
1	2	3	4	5	**8.** Everyone has input to all team decisions, rather than a few .

Chapter Ten:

Overhead Transparencies

In this chapter, you will find masters from which you can create overhead transparencies for use during your teambuilding workshops.

USING THE OVERHEAD TRANSPARENCIES

You may use the overhead transparencies in four ways :

- Key them into your word processing system "as is" or customize them to suit your specific needs .

- Photocopy the overhead transparency masters that you need from this book and use them "as is. "

- Photocopy the masters on plain paper and distribute them as handouts.

- Create flipcharts by handlettering the content on sheets of 2′ x 3′ chart paper.

The following overhead transparencies are not included in the training plans, but may be used to enhance your teambuilding training:

- *Giving Feedback to Others* (p. 257)

- *Receiving Feedback from Others* (p. 258)

- *A Decision Model* (p. 261)

TEAM MISSION

A team's mission is defined as something that the team intends to do. It is a clearly stated purpose that serves to direct and motivate team members in the pursuit of excellence.

EIGHT CRITERIA FOR EFFECTIVE MISSION STATEMENTS

- Inspirational.
- Clear and challenging.
- Differentiating.
- Stable but constantly challenged.
- Beacons and controls.
- Empowering.
- Future-oriented.
- Lived in details, not broad strokes.

MISSION FORMULATION

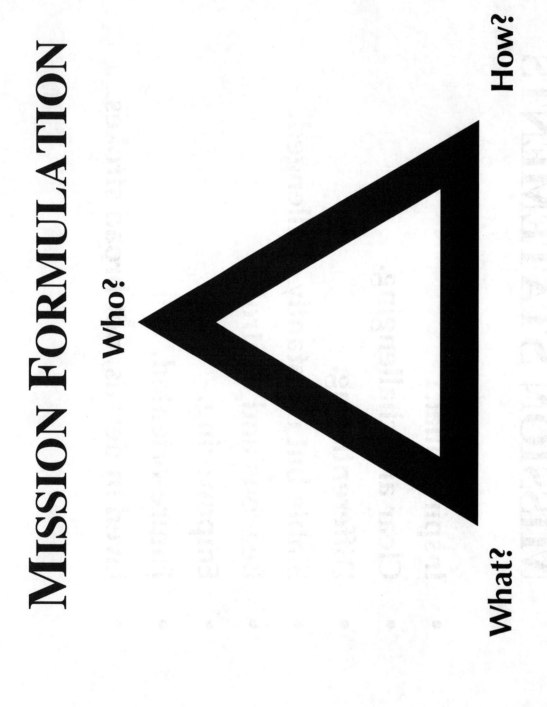

Who?

What?

How?

TEAM GOALS

Common goals provide team members with the following:

- Purpose.

- Clarity.

- Direction.

GOAL CHARACTERISTICS

- **Specific.**
- **Measurable.**
- **Attainable.**
- **Relevant.**
- **Time bound.**

STAGES OF
TEAM DEVELOPMENT

- Forming.

- Storming.

- Norming.

- Performing.

FORMING STAGE

- Excitement.

- Anxiety.

- Testing.

- Dependence.

- Trust.

STORMING STAGE

- Resistance to different approaches.

- Sharp attitude changes.

- Competitiveness and defensiveness.

- Tension and disunity.

NORMING STAGE

- Increased satisfaction.

- Developing trust and respect.

- Giving feedback to others.

- Sharing responsibilities.

- Making decisions.

PERFORMING STAGE

- **High level of interaction.**

- **Increased performance.**

- **Members are comfortable with each other.**

- **Confident and optimistic.**

243

Team Member Roles

TASK dynamics and task roles ask:

"What?" and "Why?"

PROCESS dynamics and process roles ask:

"How?"

TASK ROLES

- Information giver.
- Information seeker.
- Initiator.
- Opinion giver.
- Elaborator.
- Consensus seeker.
- Clarifier.
- Standard setter.
- Representative.

PROCESS ROLES

- Encouraging.
- Gatekeeping.
- Listening.
- Harmonizing.
- Yielding.
- Accepting.
- Supporting.

DYSFUNCTIONAL TEAM MEMBER BEHAVIORS

- Condescending.
- Bullying.
- Blocking.
- Avoiding.
- Withdrawing.
- Joking.
- Dominating.
- Self-Seeking.

RESPONSES TO DYSFUNCTIONAL BEHAVIOR

- The team provides individual counseling.

- The team confronts the individual.

- The team asks the member to leave.

COMMUNICATION PROCESS

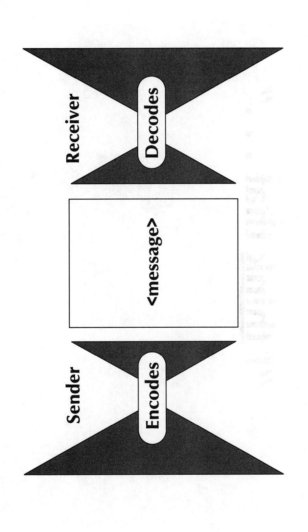

TASK COMMUNICATION

Task communication is usually introduced by the statement,

"I think that . . ."

TASK COMMUNICATION IS . . .

- Analytical.
- Auditory.
- Verbal.
- Linear.
- Concrete.
- Explicit.
- Active.

PROCESS COMMUNICATION

Process communication is introduced by the statement,

"I feel that . . . ."

PROCESS COMMUNICATION IS . . .

- Intuitive.
- Spontaneous.
- Emotional.
- Visual.
- Artistic.
- Playful.

COMMUNICATION BARRIERS

- Facts.

- Feelings.

- Values.

- Opinions.

OVERCOMING COMMUNICATION BARRIERS

Communication Channel	Phrase Response
• Facts	"The facts are . . ."
• Feelings	"I feel . . ."
• Values	"To me . . ."
• Opinions	"In my opinion . . ."

Benefits of Giving Feedback

- Feedback reduces uncertainty.

- Feedback solves problems.

- Feedback builds trust.

- Feedback strengthens relationships.

- Feedback improves work quality.

GIVING FEEDBACK TO OTHERS

- Feedback should be specific.

- Feedback should be descriptive, not evaluative.

- Feedback should be timely.

- Feedback must be on-going.

Receiving Feedback from Others

- Get as much information as possible.

- Do not become defensive.

- Use the feedback you solicit.

THE DIFFERENCE BETWEEN DECISION MAKING AND PROBLEM SOLVING

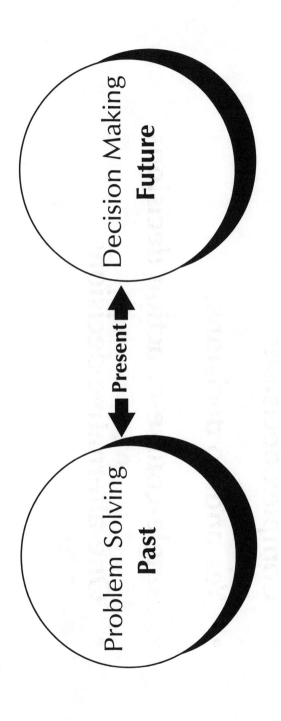

Problem Solving
Past

Present

Decision Making
Future

TYPES OF DECISIONS

- Complex decisions.

- Yes-and-no decisions.

- Single-course-of-action decisions.

- One-alternative decisions.

A DECISION MODEL

- Clarify purpose.

- Establish criteria.

- Separate criteria into two categories.

- Generate options.

- Compare options.

- Identify the risks.

- Rank risk factors.

- Make the decision.

DECISION-MAKING PROCEDURES

- Decision by authority.

- Decision by minority.

- The democratic process.

- Decision by consensus.

- Decision by unanimity.

262

PROBLEM-SOLVING STEPS

- Define the problem.

- Identify the future state.

- Identify forces.

- Analyze forces.

- Plan a strategy for change.

- Develop a plan of action.

- Implement the plan.

- Evaluate results.

CAUSES OF TEAM CONFLICT

- Personality differences.

- Values differences.

- Differences in perspective.

- Differences in goals.

- Cultural differences.

CONFLICT MANAGEMENT STRATEGIES

- Competion.

- Collaboration.

- Avoidance.

- Accommodation.

- Compromise.

COMPETITION

CONFLICT RESOLUTION APPROACH

1. When quick action is necessary.

2. When unpopular actions must be implemented.

3. When you know you are right.

4. When options are not possible.

COLLABORATION

CONFLICT RESOLUTION APPROACH

1. When you can't compromise.

2. When you are learning.

3. When you need to merge different views.

4. When you want to gain commitment.

5. When you want to improve relationships.

AVOIDANCE

CONFLICT RESOLUTION APPROACH

1. When a more important issue is pressing.

2. When you cannot satisfy your concerns.

3. When you need to let people cool down.

4. When you need more information.

5. When others can resolve the conflict more effectively.

ACCOMMODATION

CONFLICT RESOLUTION APPROACH

1. When you find that you are wrong.

2. When you want to be reasonable.

3. When issues are more important to others.

4. When you want to build social support.

5. When you want to minimize your losses.

COMPROMISE

CONFLICT RESOLUTION APPROACH

1. When goals are important but not worth it.

2. When opponents are committed to different ends.

3. When you want to achieve temporary settlements to complex issues.

4. When you want an expedient solution under time pressure.

STEPS TO MANAGING TEAM CONFLICT

1. Clarify.

2. Set goals.

3. Consider options.

4. Remove barriers.

5. Make agreements.

6. Acknowledge the solution.

SELF-AUTHORIZED TEAM LEADERSHIP

1. All team members practice some degree of self-authorized leadership.

2. Self-authorized leadership is applicable to all team members.

3. Not all team members are effective self-authorized leaders.

4. Self-authorized leadership can be developed.

BEHAVIORAL STRATEGIES

1. Self-imposed outcomes.

2. Self-management of workplace behaviors.

3. Self-observation of outcomes.

4. Self-rewards.

COGNITIVE STRATEGIES

1. Self-knowledge.

2. Individual skill.

3. Self-control.

4. Self purpose.

INCREASING LEADERSHIP EFFECTIVENESS

1. Maintain an outcome orientation.

2. Focus your attention.

3. Lead others by example.

4. Balance the mind and the heart.

275

THE SEVEN PILLARS OF LEADERSHIP CHARACTER

1. Caring.

2. Courage.

3. Honesty.

4. Integrity.

5. Responsibility.

6. Loyalty.

7. Fairness.

276

Recommended Resources

This appendix contains recommended reading that is related to teambuilding. You will find information in this appendix that will support your teambuilding knowledge-base and workshop presentation material.

RECOMMENDED RESOURCES

- Selected Bibliography

  The Selected Bibliography provides a comprehensive list of books about teambuilding by training professionals .

All the referenced books can be found in your local bookstores and libraries. The resources listed are presented for information purposes only. They do not imply any endorsement of the products or services by McGraw-Hill, American Society for Training and Development, or the author.

Selected Bibliography

Elledge, R., & Phillips, S. *Team Building for the Future*. San Diego, CA: Pfeiffer & Company, 1994.

This resource book offers trainers an overview of teambuilding, teambuilding steps, training models, facilitator roles, and tools for delivering superior training workshops.

Fisher, K. *Leading Self-Directed Work Teams*. New York, NY: McGraw-Hill, Inc., 1993.

This book explains what team leaders are and how they differ from conventional supervisors. It delivers the step-by-step guidance for getting off the endangered species list and becoming tomorrow's expert team leader. It is complete with numerous tips and checklists that summarize key concepts and strategies.

Frangos, S., with Bennett, S. *Team Zebra*. Essex Junction, VT: Oliver Wight Publications, Inc., 1993.

This book is an insider's account of how an American company turned to its people to save a vital, but failing business unit. Told as a personal narrative from the perspective of Steve Frangos, the manager of Eastman Kodak's Black and White Film Division, the book is a powerful account of a billion dollar, 100 year old business and the 1500 partners who pulled off "the turnaround of the decade."

Hunter, D., Bailey, A., & Taylor, B. *The Zen of Groups*. Auckland, New Zealand: Tandem Press, 1992.

This book shows how the effectiveness of all groups can be increased. The chapters contain the essence of effective work in groups highlighted by "Thinking Points" which help summarize the authors' informative text. It includes a "toolkit" giving 96 techniques and exercises to assist any group to move through the processes and stages to make group "synergy" a reality.

Katzenbach, J., & Smith, D. *The Wisdom of Teams*. Boston, MA: Harvard Business School Press, 1993.

This book includes dozens of stories and case examples involving real people and situations. Their accomplishments, insights, and enthusiasm are discussed as testament to the power of teams.

Kelly, M. *The Adventures of a Self-Managing Team.* San Diego, CA: Pfeiffer & Company.

This book offers a quick introduction to the team concept and its benefits, primarily for team members. It can serve as a guide for managers and consultants to help teams achieve their goals. It provides a unique look at how team members confront and deal with a variety of issues during the formation and development of the team.

Kinlaw, D. *Superior Team Development Workshop.* Amherst, MA: HRD Press, 1995.

The program is highly experiential in nature and involves participants from start to finish in assessing their team's development. It contributes to designing initiatives that will transform groups into a superior teams.

Lipnack, J. & Stamps, J. *The Team Net Factor.* Essex Junction, VT: Oliver Wight Publications, Inc., 1993.

This book provides an immediate management approach for improving private enterprise performance. Drawing on many years of experience, the authors deliver a trickle-up process of getting people educated to think for themselves in teams. It reveals how to create competitive-cooperative networks of business, institutional, and functional teams for organizational, competitive advantage.

Montebello, A. *Work Teams That Work.* Minneapolis, MN: Best Sellers Publishing, 1994.

This book provides practitioners with a thorough array of proven skills to develop teams. It contains specific steps to get teams up and running quickly or jump start teams that have lost their way.

Mullins, K. *Lessons in Teamwork: Computer Based Training Modules.* Amherst, MA: HRD Press, 1994.

This innovative software program enables you to conveniently offer interactive teambuilding training to individual team members without scheduling time consuming training sessions.

Newstrom, J. W. *The Complete Games Trainers Play.* New York, NY: McGraw-Hill, Inc., 1994.

This kit is designed to assist training professionals in program delivery. A collection of memory aids, checklists, short reference guides, planning and record keeping forms, the kit can save trainers valuable time by serving as a central resource. Rather than reinventing tools, just check the table of contents for the kit and locate ready-to-use materials for all the major aspects of preparing and refining a training program.

Parker, G., & Kropp, R. *50 Activities for Team Building.* Amherst, MA: HRD Press, 1992.

This collection of training exercises has been tested and refined in actual team training sessions and covers all aspects of team development, including mutual goal setting, managing team stagnation, and developing team norms. The activities encourage active participation and feedback from participants. It comes complete with all the necessary questionnaires, exercises, and handouts.

Pfeiffer, J. W. (editor). *The Encyclopedia of Team-Building Activities.* San Diego, CA: Pfeiffer & Company, 1991.

This resource book emphasizes teambuilding rather than team development. It is intended for the professional consultants who have experience in the HRD field. The activities in the book are representative of the kinds of issues typically addressed by teams in sensing interviews and meetings.

Scholtes, P. *The Team Handbook.* Madison. WI: Joiner Associates, Inc., 1989.

This book is a practical guide to working in or with project teams. It is packaged with step-by-step instructions, illustrations, and worksheets, all showing how to implement many quality improvement principles. It is a comprehensive, easy-to-read guide on how to use project teams to improve quality throughout an organization.

Spiegel, J., & Torres, C. *Manager's Official Guide to Team Working.* San Diego, CA: Pfeiffer & Company, 1994.

This unique handbook goes beyond definition and outlines a step-by-step model to recruit, assess, build, and facilitate a high-performing team. It is designed to be every manager's best friend when putting a team together.

Tjosvold, D. *Teamwork for Customers*. New York, NY: Jossey-Bass, Inc., 1993.

This book offers a comprehensive guide to creating customer service-driven organizations, providing advice on such tasks as assessing how well your company currently meets customer needs, earning employee support for a service-oriented vision, and using teams to implement the vision. It includes practical tips on such daily issues as solving customer grievances productively.

Torres, C. *The Tao of Teams*. San Diego, CA: Pfeiffer & Company, 1994.

This book is a poetic departure from normally analytical team literature. It applies simple, ancient wisdom to team leadership and participation. The collection of 81 thoughts and paradoxes will open readers' minds to the ways in which people form fully functioning, high-performance teams. It explores the power that is within each person and challenges all to create true meaning in their work.

Torres, C. & Spiegel, J. *Self-Directed Work Team: A Primer*. San Diego, CA: Pfeiffer & Company, 1990.

This easy to read book provides a helpful overview for team members and managers. It shows how workers can be made to feel like partners in their organizations, and how they can contribute to the improvement of products and services. It includes guiding principles, working models, key strategies, and firm action steps for implementing successful self-directed teams.

Index